Chakra Healing and the Vagus Nerve

A Beginner's Guide to Balance Energy Centers, Awaken the Nervous System and Nurture Inner Peace through Self-Healing Techniques

Isabella Harmony

Copyright Isabella Harmony 2023 - All rights reserved.

The content contained within this book may not be reproduced, duplicated, or transmitted without direct written permission from the author or the publisher.

Under no circumstances will any blame or legal responsibility be held againstthe publisher, or author, for any damages, reparation, or monetary loss due to the information contained within this book. Either directly or indirectly. Youare responsible for your own choices, actions, and results.

Legal Notice:

This book is copyright protected. This book is only for personal use. You cannot amend, distribute, sell, use, quote, or paraphrase any part, or the content within this book, without the consent of the author or publisher.

Disclaimer Notice:

Please note the information contained within this document is for educational and entertainment purposes only. All effort has been executed to present accurate, up to date, reliable, complete information. No warranties of any kind are declared or implied. Readers acknowledge that the author is not engaging in the rendering of legal, financial, medical, or professional advice. The content within this book has been derived from various sources. Please consult a licensed professional before attempting any techniques outlined in this book.

By reading this document, the reader agrees that under no circumstances is the author responsible for any losses, direct or indirect, which are incurred as a result of the use of the information contained within this document, including, but not limited to, — errors, omissions, or inaccuracies.

TABLE OF CONTENTS

Introduction 1
Chapter One: Getting To Know Your Energy 6
Chapter Two: Chakras And The Vagus Nerve 12
    Chakras And Bodily Functions 12
    A Different Kind Of Plexus 13
    What Does The Vagus Nerve Do 14
Chapter Three: The Root Chakra- Muladhara 16
    When Your Root Chakra Is Unbalanced 17
    How To Balance Your Root Chakra 18
    A Guided Meditation For The Root Chakra 25
    Affirmations For The Root Chakra 27
Chapter Four: The Sacral Chakra- Svadhisthana 28
    Signs Of An Unbalanced Sacral Chakra 29
    Helping Your Sacral Chakra 30
    A Guided Meditation For The Sacral Chakra 35
    Affirmations For The Sacral Chakra 38
Chapter Five: The Solar Plexus Chakra- Manipura 39
    How To Tell When The Solar Plexus Chakra Isn't Flowing 40
    Simple Techniques To Balance The Solar Plexus Chakra 41
    A Guided Meditation For The Solar Plexus Chakra 47
    Affirmations For The Solar Plexus Chakra 50
Chapter Six: The Heart Chakra- Anahata 52

How To Recognise A Blocked Heart Chakra............ 54

How To Heal The Heart Chakra And Embrace Love 55

A Guided Meditation For The Heart Chakra 61

Affirmations For The Heart Chakra........................ 65

Chapter Seven: The Throat Chakra- Vishuddha......... 66

What Your Throat Chakra Is Telling You................ 67

What You Can Do For Your Throat Chakra 68

A Guided Meditation For The Throat Chakra......... 74

Affirmations For The Throat Chakra 77

Chapter Eight: The Third Eye Chakra- Ajna............... 79

How To Know When The Third Eye Chakra Is Unbalanced 80

Balancing Your Third Eye Chakra............................81

A Guided Meditation For The Third Eye Chakra.... 87

Affirmations For The Third Eye Chakra 92

Chapter Nine: The Crown Chakra- Sahasrara 93

What To Expect When The Crown Chakra Is Unbalanced 94

How To Awaken Your Crown Chakra 95

A Guided Meditation For The Crown Chakra 100

Affirmations For The Crown Chakra..................... 104

Chapter Ten: Mindfulness For The Chakras And Vagus Nerve..105

Why Is Mindfulness So Popular Today..................105

Where Eastern And Western Philosophies Collide 107

    Mindful Meditation And The Vagus Nerve 108

    8 Mindful Activities 111

Chapter Eleven: A Week Of Practices To Maintain Balanced Chakras 120

    Monday 122

    Tuesday 123

    Wednesday 125

    Thursday 126

    Friday 127

    Saturday 128

    Sunday 130

Conclusion 133

References 138

Introduction

Yoga became a buzzword at least a decade ago but more recently added to the list are mindfulness and for a good reason. Even though these practices are centuries old, science and research have confirmed what Buddhists have known for years. Regular exercise of these activities has many benefits for both mental and physical health.

Speaking of which, raise your hand if your stress levels are off the chart! Each of us will have individual health concerns, but after a series of distressing global events combined with the toll of our daily responsibilities, the one thing most of us have in common is high stress levels. Stress is a crafty thing that can present itself in so many ways, some of which we don't even recognize as stress.

Tense muscles and chronic pain? Has the doctor warned you about your cholesterol levels? Are you regularly suffering from bloating or nausea? All of these symptoms could be caused by stress.

The biggest problem is that we don't take this stress seriously enough. What are the benefits of practicing yoga, mindfulness, and meditation on mental and physical health? What is the link between stress and various health conditions? How does chakra healing work and what are the benefits? Approximately 5 million deaths worldwide are attributed to mood and anxiety disorders (SingleCare, 2023). Stress has been linked to heart disease, cancer, lung ailments, and cirrhosis. Stress has also been linked to a higher risk of accidents and suicide.

If we dig a little deeper, stress can be caused by our attachment to the past and future, which causes our suffering. Yoga, mindfulness, and meditation all teach us to live more in the present and reduce stress. But I feel the burning question, where do chakras come in?

As a busy mom, it can be easy to get caught up in the chaos of daily life and neglect our spiritual and emotional needs. But through learning about the seven chakras, you can find balance and harmony in all aspects of your life.

I am a mother over 50. I spent years putting everyone else's needs and my numerous responsibilities ahead of my own. This left me feeling achy and sluggish and to be honest, concerned about my overall health. I didn't want to keep taking paracetamol for this and that and after all the hype surrounding yoga, I decided to give it a try.

This was when I first heard about chakras but my skeptical mind was having none of that. I couldn't understand how chanting a single syllable could lead to healing. And so my research began.

First off, I was relieved to discover that although stemming from Hinduism and Buddhism, chakra healing is not a religious practice but a spiritual one. This means I did no need to worry about clashes with my faith.

Whether you're new to the concept of chakras or looking to deepen your understanding, this book offers a fresh perspective from a fellow busy mum who understands the demands of daily life. Join us on this journey of self-discovery and uncover the power of your chakras.

Working to balance your chakras is a form of energy healing. The root chakra, for example, is located at the base of the spine and is associated with our sense of security and stability. The sacral chakra, located in the lower abdomen, is associated with our creativity and passion. The solar plexus chakra, located in the upper abdomen, is associated with our sense of power and self-confidence. The heart chakra, in the middle of the chest, is logically linked to love and compassion. The throat chakra, at the base of the throat, has ties to communication and self-expression. The third eye chakra, located in the center of the brow, is associated with intuition and spirituality. The crown chakra is the only chakra not associated with a physical part of the body. It is found at the top of the head and is associated with our connection to the divine, or a higher self, much like acupuncture and Reiki. There is little proven evidence of the effectiveness of energy healing but that hasn't stopped medical professionals from recommending this alternative healing method. As you are not pumping your body full of medications, chakra healing is perfectly safe, another one of my top concerns.

What makes this book unique is that we have taken a more scientific approach to the ancient practice without attempting to reinvent the wheel. When it comes to my health, I am all up for discovering alternative methods of healing but I need reassurance. For this reason, we will approach chakra healing from a more anatomical direction and discover how the vagus nerve is linked to the chakras and healing practices.

After a short time of practicing, I began to notice many positive changes. There was much less lower back pain from sitting down for too long, which enabled me to start my evening walks again. The most significant change was that I was more in tune with my physical and emotional needs so I was more able to take better care of myself. Life became lighter without the burden of stress weighing me down all the time.

Even if you don't have children, it's still more than likely that you put everybody else's priorities above your own. We live in a world where it's almost selfish to take 10 minutes for ourselves but we need to get better at changing this attitude. As the saying goes, "You can't pour from an empty cup"! While you are taking a few minutes to yourself, practice a little mindfulness coloring with the simplified symbols of each chakra at the beginning of each chapter. I don't want to stifle your creativity but try to stick to hues that represent the chakra color.

Fortunately, with a deeper understanding of the body, I was able to uncover how balancing the chakras can help the body and mind and have come to look forward to my daily sessions. For those who are doubtful like I was, we will begin with a better understanding of what energy is in terms of the chakras!

Before that, I just wanted to offer a little advice on how to get the most out of this book. For each of the chakras, you will find various yoga positions as well as a guided meditation that I have created with a specific chakra in mind. Listening to Audible books is popular nowadays but if you don't have that, there are other options. You can ask Google Assist to read the page you are on, if you are reading in PDF form, you can click on Read Out Loud, and of course, you can always simply record your own voice to playback. From personal experience, I know that yoga positions and guided meditations are better when spoken rather than read. Of course, the tone and velocity need to be relaxing so if Google Assist isn't quite as calming as you had hoped, stick to your own voice!

Without further ado, let's get back to our energy!

Chapter One:
Getting to Know Your Energy

You may have come across someone who has looked at you proclaiming that they can see your aura. As living beings, we are made up of millions of vibrating cells and as the cells move, energy is created. Imagine this field of energy as the equivalent of the atmosphere surrounding Earth. An aura refers to the energy field around a living being but chakras are more specific.

What Are Chakras

In Sanskrit, the word chakra means wheel or disk. Essentially, the chakras are wheels of energy that align with the brain and other organs. There are seven chakras, the first beginning at the base of your spine and then located up the spine to the top of the head. Each chakra is associated with an organ or gland, an emotion, as well as a color and an element. The seven chakras are:

- The root chakra- Muladhara
- The sacral chakra- Svadhisthana
- The solar plexus chakra- Manipura
- The heart chakra- Anahata
- The throat chakra- Vishuddha

- The third eye chakra- Ajna
- The crown chakra- Sahasrara

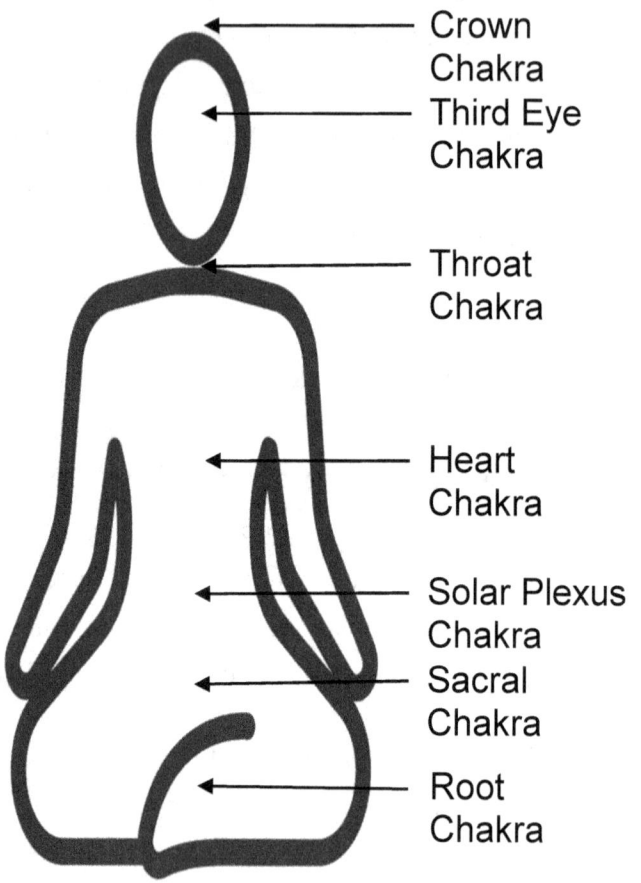

The chakra system was first mentioned in the Upanishads, sacred Hindu texts dating back to between

700 and 500 BCE. Although most people only work on the 7 main chakras, there are actually 114 disks of energy within the body. Each flow of energy is called a nadis. Where multiple nadis cross, we have a chakra. In yogic teachings, the goal is to have a balanced chakra system in order to have optimal health. When the chakras are balanced, energy can flow throughout the body, reaching the necessary organs.

It's worth mentioning that different religious teachings have their own chakra systems. Various experts have taken teachings and translations to create what is known as the New Age system. For example, the New Age system incorporates aspects of the conscious and elements but there is no mention of this in ancient Indian teachings. We will stick to the New Age system as I feel this is a more complete, spiritual approach rather than religious.

Imbalanced Energy Wheels

The chakras can be completely blocked, they can be underactive, overactive, or balanced. If they are blocked, no energy can pass through. Underactive means not enough energy can flow through compared with overactive when there is too much energy. As each corresponds to a quality, having too little energy can result in difficulties expressing that quality. Too much and the quality may dominate a person's life.

Typically, physical symptoms occur in the body close to the affected chakra. This can be anything from self-destructive behaviors like a poor diet, poor posture, particular pain in organs, and headaches or tension aches. When the chakras are unbalanced for a long period of time, physical diseases and illness can occur along with musculoskeletal problems and depression, and anxiety.

As they are all part of a system when a chakra isn't balanced, it can cause an imbalance in the others. When a chakra is unbalanced, you may notice physical and/or emotional symptoms. We will discuss each of these in more detail in the chapters.

What Can You Gain from Balancing the Chakras?

As you can imagine now, there are numerous health benefits to discovering how to balance your chakras. Here are some of my personal favorites:

- You can start to feel an overall improvement in your health and well-being.
- You can heal from physical, mental, and emotional issues much faster.
- You can discover how to be more open and aware.
- Your concentration and memory may improve.
- You can feel more positive about life without feeling like you have to fake it.
- Your creativity can begin to shine
- You may get a better night's sleep, especially when your stress is reduced.
- Your confidence, self-esteem, and sense of self-worth improve.

Why Do We Chant When Working on Our Chakras

Following the ancient traditions, Buddhists would (and still do) chant to bring greater meaning into their lives. They chant the teachings and verses that have been passed down through the generations but it's not just a form of reciting verses. Chanting helps calm the mind and prepare them for meditation. It's a daily practice that encourages calm, clarity, and concentration.

Bija mantras are those chants that are related to the chakras. In Sanskrit, bija means seed, and these are the most basic, single-syllable words that contain the essence of energy. These sounds are used for their specific vibrational frequencies with each frequency encouraging energy to a certain chakra. It sounds a little too 'out there' for some, so I like to compare chanting to sound therapy.

The benefits of sound therapy have been proven. One study on patients with fibromyalgia showed that 10 sessions of low-frequency sound stimulation reduced pain and improved sleep. Nearly three-quarters of the participants were able to reduce their pain medication (Naghdi, et. al., 2015).

We will discuss each of these seed mantras in the chapters dedicated to one of the seven chakras. And there will be a little more science to help see how chanting can bring about healing before this.

As you work on balancing your chakras, visualization is going to help a great deal and this will also help your mind stay focused. Try to visualize the wheel of energy that you are working on, picture it as its related color and as you are chanting, imagine those vibrations moving towards the center of the wheel. Visualization may sound a bit far-fetched but the brain has no way of telling what is real and what is imaginary. Telling your brain that energy is flowing to the area you are directing it can lead to greater results.

For many, diving into chakra healing can lead to the sense that something is too good to be true. For those who aren't convinced just yet, I completely understand. That is why we have just one more short chapter to link the old worlds with the new and see things from the perspective of science.

Chapter Two:
Chakras and the Vagus Nerve

This is the science bit that I really love. This is when chakra healing really made sense to me.

Starting with the vagus nerve, our autonomic nervous system is made up of the sympathetic nervous system (SNS) and the parasympathetic nervous system (PNS). When faced with stress, the sympathetic nervous system kicks in and our body goes into fight or flight mode. This is often a good thing because it prepares the body for action. However, chronic stress and the sympathetic nervous system being too active can cause havoc on our circulatory system, immune system, brain function, and even our digestive system.

After a stressor, it can take the body anywhere from 20 minutes to 60 minutes for the parasympathetic nervous system to return the body to its normal 'rest and digest' state. During this time, hormones are still rushing around the body and the impact of stress is still in play.

The vagus nerve is the longest of the cranial nerves and starts at the base of your brain, passing the vocal cords where it then starts to branch out to the organs in your body, all the way down to your gut. We will come back to the vagus nerve after diving into our organs, glands, and nerves!

Chakras and Bodily Functions

Although we will look at physical and emotional symptoms in each chapter, I wanted to keep the physiological side of the chakras together with the vagus nerve because of the correlation. Here are how the chakras relate to various glands and organs in the body, mainly because of their location.

- The root chakra- the reproductive organs (testes or ovaries)
- The sacral chakra- the adrenal glands (the immune system and metabolism)
- The Solar Plexus- the pancreas (regulates metabolism)
- The heart chakra- the thymus glands (the immune system)
- The throat chakra- the thyroid gland (regulates body temperature and metabolism)
- The third eye chakra- the pineal gland (biological systems and sleep)
- The crown chakra- the pituitary gland (produces hormones and controls the other glands)

A Different Kind of Plexus

Within the body, we have various nerve bundles, also known as a plexus. There are two important subdivisions of plexuses that relate to our healing. Along the spine, there are five. Starting at the base, we have the coccygeal plexus. The sacral plexus is where the sciatic nerve comes from. The lumbar plexus is important for the muscles and skin in the hips whereas the brachial plexus contains nerves that communicate with the chest, shoulders, and arms. Finally, the cervical plexus is at the top of the spinal cord and has the nerves that are in the back of the head.

As previously mentioned, visualization is a wonderful practice when healing chakras. I like to visualize my spine and these nerve bundles that are uncoincidentally in line with the chakras.

As well as these spinal plexuses, there are autonomic plexuses that contain fibers from the PSN and the SNS. The celiac plexus is behind the pancreas and sends signals from the brain to the digestive organs. The collection of nerves from the esophagus to the rectum is called Auerbach's plexus and is responsible for the movement of food through the digestive system. This nerve bundle works with Meissner's plexus in the intestinal wall. The pharyngeal plexus helps with the swallowing action and is found near the pharynx. We also have the pelvic plexus involved in the reproductive system and finally, the cardiac plexus supplies nerves to the heart.

What Does the Vagus Nerve Do

Imagine the vagus nerve as the highway to all of these nerve bundles and this amazing nerve contains 75 percent of the parasympathetic nerve fibers. After passing the throat, the vagus nerve branches into the heart, lungs, liver, gallbladder, spleen, pancreas, and both intestines. It also branches into the kidneys, bladder, uterus, ovaries, penis, and scrotum. This means it plays a role in bodily functions such as:

- Heart rate
- Immune response
- Breathing rate
- Blood pressure
- Digestion

- Frequency of urination
- Mood
- Muscle and skin sensations
- Speech
- Taste
- Mood

Tieing all this together, each cell in the human body vibrates. These vibrations are so small that they can only be detected with atomic force microscopes yet these vibrations generate electromagnetic energy, and this includes all of our nerve cells! This energy has the ability to change cells and therefore, body functions.

There has been a lot of research on vagus nerve stimulation and its impact on the body. Now that you understand the extent of the nervous system and the role it plays in our health, you can see the importance of improving the vagal tone. There are various ways to stimulate the vagus nerve so the parasympathetic nervous system can return the body to normal faster, one method is singing or humming. So, you can start to see how chanting can help heal the vagus nerve and therefore healing. Another way is through deep breathing, a key part of yoga and meditation!

On that note, it's time to get straight into the first chakra at the very base of our spine, the root chakra.

Chapter Three:
The Root Chakra- Muladhara

The root chakra is the base of our physical body and is found at the very base of the spine. The word Muladhara is composed of mula meaning "root" and dhara meaning "base". This chakra is related to the earth element and is the first chakra, making it the foundation for the balance of the other chakras.

Apana Prana is centered around the root chakra and this vital force is responsible for removing toxins from the body. At the same time, this chakra replaces the earth element in the body. Without this, the body can suffer from physical and mental diseases. Due to its location, this chakra is responsible for keeping us grounded and connected to Earth. It is linked to our primal needs, stability, and support.

The chakra is associated with the color red. It is represented by a four-petalled lotus flower, each petal representing one of earth's elements: earth, water, fire, and air. When combined, they form prakriti, or the whole physical world.

When Your Root Chakra Is Unbalanced

If your root chakra is unbalanced, you may have trouble sleeping and fatigue, a weaker immune system, changes in weight, lower back issues, and problems with legs, knees, and feet. In terms of emotions, it's possible that you will feel unsafe or unstable, your behavior might be erratic, or you may have a lack of motivation. There could be a level of anxiety. You may feel dissociated from the world and your outlook can often be negative. On a spiritual level, you may be doubting your place in the world.

Some of the symptoms of a blocked root chakra are the same, such as disconnection and anxiety. Physical pain may be felt in the same areas and there may be some digestive disorders too. Anxiety might reach a level where panic attacks occur along with self-pity and depression.

Some people feel a need to hold on to material things, even hoarding. There is a greed for money and material things, perhaps a subconscious need to fill a void that needs to be filled with the earth element.

Because this chakra has a strong relationship with survival, stress can unbalance it and continuous stress could lead to a blocked root chakra. Trauma, chronic stress, or high levels of stress cause a rush of cortisol (the stress hormone) as the body prepares for fight or flight.

When the root chakra is holding on to too much energy, the fixation with material things can turn into addictions. Behavior may be dominant, even aggressive. You might notice you are overeating, you are constantly on edge, or you are paranoid.

On the other hand, when your root chakra is balanced, you will feel centered and secure in the present moment. You will feel safe and supported, strong and at peace. You will be comfortable with your body and you will know that all of your basic needs are being met.

Balancing your chakras isn't a magic solution for removing all the stress in your life. But when you start working on balancing the root chakra, you will notice a change in your relationship with stress.

How to Balance Your Root Chakra

As yoga and chakra healing go hand in hand, we will start with yoga poses that specifically look to the root chakra, opening it up so that energy can flow through the body but also, so that any pent-up energy causing the chakra to be overactive can be released.

Corpse Pose (Shavasana)

1. Lie down on your back on a yoga mat or a comfortable surface. Ensure that your spine is straight and aligned with the floor.
2. Keep your legs straight and slightly apart, and your arms relaxed by your sides with your palms facing upwards.
3. Close your eyes and breathe deeply, inhaling and exhaling through your nose. Allow your body to

relax completely and release any tension from your muscles.
4. Focus your attention on your breath and let go of any thoughts or distractions that come to your mind.
5. Stay in this position for a few minutes or as long as you like, ideally at least 5-10 minutes.

Sun Salutations (Surya Namaskara)

1. Start by standing at the front of your mat with your feet together and your hands at your heart center in prayer position.
2. Inhale and raise your arms above your head, looking up at your hands.
3. Exhale and bend forward. Bring your hands down to the floor beside your feet. If need be, keep your knees slightly bent.
4. Inhale and step your right foot back into a lunge position, keeping your left knee bent and your hands on the mat on either side of your left foot.
5. Exhale and step your left foot back to plank pose, with your arms straight and your hands shoulder-width apart.
6. Lower your body down to the floor, keeping your elbows close to your sides and your hands near your shoulders.
7. Inhale and raise your chest up into upward-facing dog pose, with your arms straight and your shoulders down.
8. Exhale and lift your hips up into downward-facing dog pose, with your arms straight and your feet hip-width apart. Remain here for a few breaths.

9. Inhale and step your right foot forward into a lunge position, keeping your left knee on the floor.
10. Exhale and step your left foot forward to meet your right foot, bending forward into a forward fold.
11. Inhale and raise your arms above your head, looking up at your hands.
12. Exhale and bring your hands into prayer position.

Child's Pose (Shashankasana)

1. Start on your hands and knees with your wrists directly under your shoulders and your knees hip-width apart.
2. Inhale and lengthen your spine, reaching the crown of your head forward and your tailbone back.
3. Exhale and lower your hips back towards your heels, bringing your forehead to the floor.
4. Extend your arms forward, resting your hands on the floor, or bring your hands back by your sides with your palms facing up.
5. Relax your shoulders down and back and allow your entire body to sink into the pose.
6. Breathe deeply and smoothly, focusing on the sensation of the breath moving in and out of your body.
7. Hold the pose for a few breaths, or as long as you like.

8. To come out of the pose, slowly walk your hands back towards your knees, then gently come up to a seated position.

Garland Pose (Malasana)

1. Start by standing at the front of your mat with your feet hip-width apart and your arms at your sides.
2. Inhale and raise your arms above your head, then exhale and bend your knees, coming into a squatting position.
3. Keep your feet flat on the floor and your heels slightly lifted if needed. You can also place a folded blanket or block under your heels for support.
4. Bring your hands together in prayer position at your heart center and use your elbows to gently press your knees apart.
5. Keep your spine straight and your chest lifted, and gaze forward or slightly upwards.
6. Breathe deeply and smoothly, holding the pose for a few breaths or as long as you like.
7. To come out of the pose, release your hands to the floor, straighten your legs, and come up to a standing position.

Warrior II (Virabhadrasana II)

1. Begin in Tadasana (Mountain Pose) at the front of your mat, with your arms at your sides and your feet hip-width apart.

2. Step your left foot back about 3-4 feet, turning your left foot out at a 90-degree angle, and keeping your right foot facing forward.
3. Align your front heel with the arch of your back foot and ensure that your feet are firmly rooted into the ground.
4. Inhale and raise your arms to shoulder height. Keep your palms facing down.
5. Exhale and bend your right knee, keeping it directly over your ankle, and extend your left leg straight behind you.
6. Keep your hips facing forward and your shoulders relaxed, gazing out over your right fingertips.
7. Hold the pose for a few breaths, or as long as you like.
8. To come out of the pose, straighten your right leg, bring your arms down to your sides, and step your left foot forward to meet your right foot.
9. Repeat the sequence on the other side, stepping your right foot back and bending your left knee.

Tree Pose (Vrkshasana)

1. Begin in Tadasana (Mountain Pose) at the front of your mat, with your arms at your sides and your feet hip-width apart.
2. Shift your weight onto your left foot, and lift your right foot off the ground, placing the sole of your right foot on the inside of your left thigh. Make sure your right knee is pointing out to the side.

3. Press your right foot into your left thigh and bring your hands together in prayer position at your heart center.
4. Keep your gaze fixed on a point in front of you to help with balance.
5. Breathe deeply and smoothly, holding the pose for a few breaths, or as long as you like.
6. To come out of the pose, release your hands to your sides, and slowly lower your right foot to the ground.
7. Repeat the sequence on the other side, shifting your weight onto your right foot and placing the sole of your left foot on the inside of your right thigh.

Mountain Pose (Tadasana)

1. Stand tall at the front of your mat, with your feet hip-width apart, and your arms at your sides.
2. Distribute your weight evenly across both feet, grounding down through your toes, arches, and heels.
3. Engage your leg muscles, lifting your kneecaps, and engaging your thighs.
4. Lengthen your spine, lift your chest, and draw your shoulders down and back.
5. Relax your arms, allowing them to hang naturally at your sides, with your palms facing forward.
6. Soften your gaze, and focus on your breath, taking slow and steady inhales and exhales.
7. Hold the pose for a few breaths, or as long as you like.

8. To come out of the pose, gently release any tension in your body, and slowly lower your arms to your sides.

If you aren't keen on yoga, there are other physical activities that can help balance the root chakra. Walking barefoot in nature (even if it's just your garden) and gardening can make a difference. A practice known as earthing involves direct contact with the earth in order to use the natural electric charges of the earth to restore the body.

Crystals can also hold vibrational energy that can lead to healing. Those that can help your root chakra are more often red and black. Some examples can include:

- Obsidian
- Hematite
- Onyx
- Bloodstone
- Red Jasper
- Black Tourmaline
- Garnet
- Smoky Quartz

Essential oils can be used during meditation or visualization. But they don't need to be saved for a specific practice. When choosing essential oils for your root chakra, aim for earth-scented oils like cedarwood, rosemary, sandalwood, basil, and patchouli.

Finally, you can literally feed your root chakra with earth elements by adding more root vegetables to your diet. This includes potatoes, garlic, onions, carrots, parsnips, and beets. Red berries may also help.

A Guided Meditation for the Root Chakra

Find a comfortable position, either sitting or lying down, and allow yourself to shake off any stress and tension as you start to relax. Close your eyes and take a deep breath in, and as you exhale, let go of any final stress or tension that is weighing you down.

As we start our journey of healing and balancing our root chakra, let's begin by focusing on our breath. Take a slow, deep breath in through your nose, filling your lungs with fresh, rejuvenating air. Hold it for a moment, and then slowly exhale through your mouth, releasing any negativity from your body.

Now, let's bring our attention to the base of your spine to your root chakra. Visualize a vibrant, glowing red light at the base of your spine, releasing warmth and stability. This red light represents the energy of your root chakra, connecting you to the earth and providing you with a strong foundation.

Take a moment to become aware of any sensations in this area. Notice if there are any areas of tension or blockages. With each breath, imagine this red light expanding and growing brighter, nourishing and healing your root chakra.

As you continue to breathe deeply, imagine roots extending from the base of your spine, reaching deep into the earth. Feel these roots grounding you, anchoring you to the earth's core. Sense the stability and strength that comes from this connection.

Now, imagine yourself standing in a beautiful natural setting, surrounded by the elements of nature. Feel the solid ground beneath your feet, the gentle breeze brushing against your skin, and the warmth of the sun shining upon you. Allow yourself to become fully present in this moment, connecting deeply with the earth.

As you stand in this serene place, affirm to yourself, "I am safe. I am secure. I am rooted." Repeat this affirmation several times, allowing its positive energy to permeate every cell of your being.

Take a few moments to reflect on any areas of your life where you may feel a lack of stability or insecurity. Visualize these challenges as heavy stones or burdens that you are carrying. With each breath, imagine these stones becoming lighter and lighter until they eventually dissolve into the earth beneath your feet. Feel a sense of release and liberation as you let go of these burdens, allowing yourself to fully embrace a sense of security and stability.

Now, bring your attention back to the red light at the base of your spine. Visualize it spinning and glowing with vitality. Feel its warmth and energy radiating throughout your entire body, bringing balance and harmony to your root chakra.

As we conclude this meditation, take a moment to express gratitude for the grounding energy of your root chakra and for the connection you have established with the earth. Know that you can return to this meditation whenever you need to restore balance and stability in your life.

Gently bring your awareness back to your breath. Take a few deep breaths in and out, gradually becoming more present in your surroundings. When you're ready, slowly open your eyes, carrying the sense of grounding and stability with you into your day.

Remember, you are rooted, you are secure, and you are always supported by the loving energy of the earth.

Affirmations for the Root Chakra

When you are using mantras and affirmations, try to visualize your root chakra as a ball of red energy. As you breathe in, imagine the warmth of the breath as red energy flows to your root chakra.

In chakra healing, Sanskrit has a set of 'bija' or seed mantras. These are one-syllable sounds that are specific to each chakra. This is because the sound produced creates a vibration that balances that particular chakra. The mantra for the root chakra is *lam*. There are also affirmations you can repeat several times throughout the day to promote chakra healing. Here are some examples:

- I have abundance in life
- I am at peace
- I have deep roots
- I feel safe and secure
- I am right where I am meant to be
- At this moment, I am stable and grounded
- I feel protected
- I am at home in my body
- I am strong, steady, and well
- All of my needs are met

Once you begin working on your root chakra and start to notice the difference, you know that energy can now flow to the path of the next chakra.

Chapter Four:
The Sacral Chakra- Svadhisthana

Found in the lower abdomen, the purpose of the Sacral Charka is movement and connection. Translated it means sweetness. It is linked to the element of water, relevant because this chakra plays a role in our bodily fluids and the color orange.

The sacral chakra is tied to our pleasure, creativity, and how we express our creativity. With the location so close to the reproductive organs, it has also been called the sex chakra and plays a role in our sensuality and sexuality. It is also related to the divine feminine. Kundalini energy (meaning coiled in Sanskrit) is the divine feminine energy that sits within all of us at the base of the spine. Working on the sacral chakra can awaken Kundalini energy for physical, emotional, and spiritual benefits.

The symbol of the sacral chakra is a six-petalled lotus, governed by Parvati, the Hindu goddess of power, fertility, and fidelity. For this reason, the chakra is often associated with relationships and intimacy.

Signs of an Unbalanced Sacral Chakra

If your sacral chakra is unbalanced, you may struggle with creativity but this could be in very subtle forms like not remembering your dreams. There may also be low libido, a lack of desire, or a fear of pleasure. There could be some insecurity, especially in relationships. Some will experience codependency. There might be difficulties with emotions and more so with the inner child, the part of our subconscious that holds on to both the good and the bad memories. It's possible that the boundaries within a relationship are too rigid.

Physical symptoms can also be related to lower back and hip issues along with other joint pain and arthritis. Problems with kidneys can be associated with this chakra and so can sexual health, including premenstrual conditions. Some people have difficulties experiencing emotional or sexual intimacy.

When the sacral chakra is overactive, the boundaries in a relationship are weak or nonexistent. It's common to feel complete dissatisfaction with life and this comes out in extreme mood swings. To the real extreme, some are over-the-top with their affection and they may not have full control over their sexual desires. Mood swings can also make some people feel like they are drawing in their own emotions because they are so strong.

A balanced sacral chakra allows for emotional awareness, making emotional intelligence easier to achieve. You will feel more connected with yourself and the world and creativity will come easily to you. There will be a passion for life and a healthy sex drive.

Helping Your Sacral Chakra

Remember that you don't need to get the yoga pants on or go to a class. Just waking up and spending 10 to 15 minutes in the morning doing a few poses can make a world of difference.

Crow Pose (Kakasana)

1. Begin in Tadasana (Mountain Pose) at the front of your mat, with your arms at your sides and your feet hip-width apart.
2. Step your left foot back about 3-4 feet, turning your left foot out at a 90-degree angle, and keeping your right foot facing forward.
3. Align your front heel with the arch of your back foot and ensure that your feet are firmly rooted into the ground.
4. Inhale and raise your arms to shoulder height, with your palms facing down.
5. Exhale and bend your right knee, keeping it directly over your ankle, and extend your left leg straight behind you.
6. Keep your hips facing forward and your shoulders relaxed, gazing out over your right fingertips.
7. Hold the pose for a few breaths, or as long as you like.
8. To come out of the pose, straighten your right leg, bring your arms down to your sides, and step your left foot forward to meet your right foot.
9. Repeat the sequence on the other side, stepping your right foot back and bending your left knee.

Classical Triangle Pose (Trikonasana)

1. Begin by standing straight with your feet about 3 to 4 feet apart, with the toes of your right foot pointing to the right and the toes of your left foot pointing slightly inward.
2. Raise both arms to shoulder height, parallel to the floor, with your palms facing down.
3. While inhaling, lengthen your spine and exhale as you extend your torso to the right side, reaching your right hand down towards your right ankle. Make sure to keep both legs straight and engage your core muscles to maintain balance.
4. Rest your right hand on your ankle, shin, or the floor outside your right foot, and extend your left arm straight up towards the ceiling, with your palm facing forward.
5. Turn your head to look up at your left hand and hold this position for 5 to 10 deep breaths.
6. To come out of the pose, inhale and raise your left arm up towards the ceiling as you straighten your torso, then exhale and lower your arms to your sides.
7. Repeat the pose on the other side by turning your feet to the left and reaching your left hand down towards your left ankle.

Side Plank Pose (Vashishtasana)

1. Begin with your hands shoulder-width apart but your feet together.

2. Shift your weight onto your right hand and rotate your body to the right, stacking your left foot on top of your right foot.
3. Lift your left arm up towards the ceiling, keeping it in line with your shoulder, and engage your core muscles to maintain balance.
4. Keep your body in a straight line from your head to your heels, with your gaze towards your raised hand.
5. Hold this pose for 30 seconds to 1 minute, then slowly lower yourself back to the starting position.
6. Repeat the pose on the other side by shifting your weight onto your left hand and stacking your right foot on top of your left foot, while lifting your right arm toward the ceiling.

Camel Pose (Ustrasana)

1. Begin by kneeling on the floor with your knees hip-width apart and your shins and feet flat on the floor.
2. Place your hands on your lower back with your fingers pointing downwards and your elbows close to your body.
3. Inhale and lift your chest up towards the ceiling, lengthening your spine and arching your back.
4. As you exhale, lean back slowly, bringing your hands to your heels or the back of your thighs.
5. Keep your neck in a neutral position or allow it to drop back, but only if it is comfortable for you.
6. Hold this pose for 5 to 10 deep breaths, then slowly return to the starting position.

Bound Angle Pose (Baddha Konasana)

1. Begin by sitting on the floor with your legs straight out in front of you.
2. Bend your knees, then bring the soles of your feet together. Allow your knees to drop to the sides.
3. Hold onto your ankles or feet with your hands, and gently draw your heels towards your groin.
4. Use your elbows to press your knees down towards the floor, while keeping your spine straight and your shoulders relaxed.
5. Hold this pose for 30 seconds to 1 minute, while taking deep breaths and allowing your body to relax.
6. Release the pose by gently releasing your feet and extending your legs in front of you.

Reverse Warrior (Viparita Vibhadrasana)

1. Begin in Warrior II Pose, with your right foot forward and your left foot back.
2. Turn your left foot slightly inwards and reach your right arm up towards the ceiling, keeping your right knee bent and your left leg straight.
3. As you inhale, reach your right arm back and over your head towards the left side of the room, while keeping your left hand on your left thigh for support.
4. Keep your chest and hips open towards the side of the room, and gaze towards your raised hand.
5. Hold this pose for 5 to 10 deep breaths, then release by bringing your right hand down to your right thigh and returning to Warrior II Pose.

6. Repeat the pose on the other side, with your left foot forward and your right foot back.

Dancing Goddess (Utkata Konasana)

1. Begin in Mountain Pose, standing tall with your feet hip-distance apart and your arms at your sides.
2. Shift your weight onto your left foot, and bring your right heel towards your right buttock, reaching back with your right hand to hold onto your right ankle.
3. As you inhale, lift your left arm up towards the ceiling, and begin to shift your weight onto your left foot.
4. As you exhale, begin to kick your right foot back and up, extending your right arm forward.
5. Keep your chest lifted and your gaze forward and try to maintain your balance.
6. Hold this pose for 5 to 10 deep breaths, then release the pose and repeat on the other side.

Dancing is a wonderful way to bring more energy to your sacral chakra. From a logical point of view, dancing opens the hips but from experience, at least personal experience, dancing makes you feel good, dare I say even a little sexy. You don't need to be any good at it, just put on your favorite tunes and start shaking your hips!

One of the best crystals for the sacral chakra is the moonstone. It helps to develop a stronger connection with the energy of the divine feminine. It also has a way of helping us to balance our needs with our wants. You may want to look out for:

- Tiger's eye
- Carnelian
- Autumn jasper
- Carnelian
- Mookaite
- Orange Calcite
- Sunstone

If you are interested in using essential oils for the sacral chakra, sandalwood, jasmine, clary sage, pink pepper seed, massoia bark, and jasmine are lovely options. Bear in mind that essential oils will only be beneficial if you like the smell. I know so many people who force themselves to inhale lavender because it "relaxes them" but their hate for the smell just stresses them out even more.

Some foods that may help are not only orange but also quite high in water content, for example, peach, mango, and mandarins. Oysters have often been seen as an aphrodisiac and other foods are related to the sacral chakra because of their connection with fertility- seeds and foods with many seeds.

A Guided Meditation for the Sacral Chakra

Gently close your eyes and take a few deep breaths, bringing yourself completely to this present moment. Feel the weight of your body being supported by the earth beneath you, grounding you into the present.

As you continue to breathe deeply, bring your attention to the area just below your navel and your sacral chakra. Visualize a vibrant, glowing orange light in this area, radiating warmth and energy. Imagine this light expanding and filling your entire lower abdomen, infusing your sacral chakra with vitality and balance.

Now, imagine a gentle flame at the base of your spine, representing your Kundalini energy. Imagine this flame beginning to rise, slowly and gracefully, as it travels up your spine. Feel its warmth and power as it moves through each energy center, energizing and awakening them along the way.

As the Kundalini flame reaches your sacral chakra, feel a surge of passion and creativity wash over you. This energy center is associated with the element of water, and its flow and fluidity represent the realm of emotions, sensuality, and pleasure. Allow yourself to connect with these qualities as you continue to breathe deeply, feeling the energy of the sacral chakra expanding and harmonizing within you.

Now, let us explore the concept of intimacy. Intimacy starts with yourself. Take a moment to reflect on your relationship with yourself. Are you kind and nurturing towards yourself? Do you honor your needs and desires? Breathe into any areas of self-neglect or self-judgment, and with each breath, release any feelings of unworthiness or self-doubt.

As you breathe, imagine a warm, healing light flowing into your sacral chakra, melting away any barriers or blockages that hinder your ability to connect intimately with yourself. Visualize these barriers dissolving, and a loving acceptance of yourself taking their place. Embrace the understanding that you are deserving of love, pleasure, and joy.

Now, envision this loving energy expanding outward, extending to your relationships with others. Think about your boundaries, which are essential for healthy and fulfilling connections. Reflect on your current relationships and how they align with your needs, beliefs, and values. Notice if there are any areas where you may need to establish or reinforce your boundaries.

Take a moment to set an intention to honor your own boundaries while respecting the boundaries of others. Visualize yourself standing firm in your values and expressing your needs with clarity and compassion. See your relationships flourishing as you navigate them with openness and respect.

Now, as you focus on the sacral chakra, feel the energy of intimacy and healthy boundaries intertwining within you. Allow this energy to flow freely, harmonizing your connection with yourself and others. Feel the warmth of intimacy filling your entire body, radiating love and acceptance.

Take a few moments to breathe deeply and soak in this transformative energy. Know that you have the power to cultivate deep connections, both with yourself and those around you. Trust in your ability to create fulfilling relationships based on love, respect, and healthy boundaries.

When you are ready, gently bring your awareness back to your physical body. Wiggle your fingers and toes, and slowly open your eyes. Take a moment to appreciate the energy you have cultivated within your sacral chakra. Remember to take the energy you have created and use it when you need to balance and nurture your connection with intimacy and relationship boundaries.

Affirmations for the Sacral Chakra

The seed mantra for the sacral chakra is *vam*. There is no need to really exaggerate the v sound but it's nice to take advantage of the more noticeable vibration. Close your eyes for a few minutes and practice the sound, mentally sending those vibrations to your lower abdomen. Here are some affirmations to improve the balance in your sacral chakra.

- I deserve all the pleasure in my life
- I move freely and effortlessly
- Life is pleasurable
- I have boundaries that protect me
- I am a creative being
- My emotions are balanced
- It's safe to express my sexuality
- I am playful
- My creativity feeds my soul
- I let go of the emotions that no longer have a purpose
- I breathe in energizing, golden light.

Without feeling any rush to move on, once your sacral chakra is flowing freely, it's time to discover what is happening a little further up in your body.

Chapter Five:
The Solar Plexus Chakra- Manipura

Our third energy wheel is approximately four fingers up from your belly button and is associated with the element of fire. I love the translation of this chakra. Mani means shining gem and pura means place, so you can imagine your Solar Plexus as the place of the shining gem.

The solar plexus chakra holds samana prana energy. This is the energy of digestion and how we absorb nutrients, taking energy from the sun and food containing heat. It is responsible for bringing you warmth and light, just like how you would feel after spending some time outdoors on a beautiful sunny day. It also has a link to our intellect, ego, willpower, and sometimes aggression. This makes sense considering the power of fire. Working on this chakra is important for body and mind balance.

This chakra is represented by a triangle inside a lotus flower. Each of the 10 petals of the lotus flower represents a negative quality that we need to overcome to balance the chakra:

1. Spiritual ignorance
2. Fear
3. Jealousy
4. Betrayal
5. Shame
6. Thirst
7. Disgust
8. Delusion
9. Foolishness
10. Sadness

The triangle in the lotus flower is pointing down and is the symbol of fire.

How to Tell When the Solar Plexus Chakra Isn't Flowing

When the solar plexus chakra is underactive, you will probably suffer from poor digestion such as indigestion, heartburn, ulcers, and weight gain. Emotionally, you may suffer from low self-esteem and self-trust. This can often cause 'analysis paralysis' to be overthinking to the point where nothing gets done, which has a knock-on effect on your motivation. Some people have a victim mentality when energy isn't flowing properly and it is difficult for them to take responsibility.

If the chakra is blocked, the digestion issues become more serious, possibly with eating disorders, diabetes, and problems with the pancreas, liver, and/or colon.

There may be an obsessive need to control angry outbursts. This can also be said for when the solar plexus chakra is overactive but there is a greater need to be right and competitive. Overactivity in this area can lead to people becoming self-centered, narrow-minded, and hyperactive. In some cases, sedatives are appealing to overcome this hyperactivity.

Those who have a balanced solar plexus chakra can enjoy self-confidence and clarity in who they are and their purpose in life. They have goals and the resilience to achieve them. This enables them to make better decisions and they have the right frame of mind to know when to take risks. Because their digestive system is functioning as it should, they have a healthy metabolism and plenty of energy.

Simple Techniques to Balance the Solar Plexus Chakra

Once again, we will start with the yoga poses. The reason I love yoga so much is that as I sit here at my desk for a few hours I start to feel a bit sluggish. All it takes is for me to stand up and do a couple of poses to stretch out my body and feel the rush of blood, and energy to parts that have me still for too long. Give it a try!

Cobra Pose (Bhujangasana)

1. Lie down on your stomach, with your legs extended behind you and your toes flat on the floor. Place your hands on the floor, palms down, next to your shoulders.
2. Inhale and slowly lift your head, chest, and shoulders off the ground, keeping your elbows

close to your body. Your hands should still be on the floor, supporting your upper body.

3. Hold the pose for a few breaths, while keeping your gaze forward and your shoulders relaxed. Do not strain your neck or push yourself too far.
4. To release the pose, exhale and lower your upper body back down to the ground, relaxing your arms and shoulders.

Reverse Plank (Puvottanasana)

1. Begin by sitting on the floor with your legs extended in front of you, feet flexed and palms resting on the ground behind you, fingers pointing towards your feet.
2. Press your palms and feet firmly into the ground and lift your hips off the ground. Your body should be in a straight line from your head, through your spine, to your heels.
3. Keep your arms straight and engaged, shoulders down and away from your ears, and chest lifted. Keep your gaze straight ahead.
4. Hold the pose for a few breaths, gradually increasing the duration with practice.
5. To release the pose, slowly lower your hips back down to the ground and rest.

Boat Pose (Navasana)

1. Sit on the mat with your legs extended in front of you and your hands resting on the ground beside your hips.
2. Lean back slightly and lift your feet off the ground, keeping your knees bent.

3. Slowly straighten your legs, so your body forms a V-shape. Keep your chest lifted, and your shoulders relaxed.
4. Extend your arms forward alongside your legs, keeping them parallel to the floor. If possible, straighten your legs fully, but do not strain.
5. Hold the pose for a few breaths, engaging your core muscles and maintaining your balance.
6. To release the pose, exhale and lower your feet and hands back to the ground.

Dolphin Pose (Adha Pincha Mayurasana)

1. Start in a tabletop position with your hands and knees on the mat, with your palms shoulder-width apart, and your fingers spread wide.
2. Lower your forearms to the floor, keeping your elbows directly under your shoulders and your arms parallel to each other. Keep your palms facing down.
3. Tuck your toes and lift your hips up towards the ceiling, forming an inverted V-shape with your body.
4. Press your forearms and palms firmly into the floor, and lift your head and neck off the ground, keeping your gaze between your hands.
5. Keep your legs straight and engaged, with your heels reaching towards the ground. If necessary, you can bend your knees slightly.
6. Hold the pose for a few breaths, focusing on deep breathing and engaging your core muscles.
7. To release the pose, slowly lower your knees to the floor and rest in Child's Pose.

Cat Cow Pose (Bitilasana Marjaryasana)

1. Begin on your hands and knees in a tabletop position, with your wrists directly under your shoulders and your knees directly under your hips.
2. Inhale and gently arch your back, lifting your head and tailbone towards the ceiling. This is the Cow Pose.
3. Exhale and round your spine, tucking your chin towards your chest and bringing your tailbone towards your knees. This is the Cat Pose.
4. Repeat the sequence, flowing smoothly between the Cow Pose and the Cat Pose with each inhale and exhale.
5. Continue the sequence for several breaths, allowing your movements to become fluid and synchronized with your breath.
6. If desired, you can also add variations to the sequence, such as moving your hips in circles or adding gentle twists.
7. To release the pose, return to the neutral tabletop position, and rest in Child's Pose or any other comfortable posture.

Snake Pose (Bhujangasana)

1. Start by lying face down on the mat with your palms resting on the floor beside your shoulders and your elbows close to your sides.
2. Engage your core muscles and press your pubic bone into the floor.
3. Inhale and slowly lift your chest and head off the ground, using your back muscles to support the

movement. Keep your elbows near your sides and your shoulders free from tension.
4. Keep your gaze forward or slightly upward and avoid straining your neck.
5. Hold the pose for a few breaths, breathing deeply and relaxing your shoulders.
6. To release the pose, exhale and lower your chest and head back to the ground.

Upward Salute Side Bend Pose (Urdhva Hastasana variation)

1. Begin in a standing position, with your feet hip-distance apart and your arms by your sides.
2. Inhale and lift your arms overhead, reaching towards the sky, with your palms facing each other.
3. Keep your shoulders relaxed, and your gaze forward or slightly upward.
4. Exhale and bend your upper body to the right, reaching your right hand towards the floor and your left hand towards the sky.
5. Keep your hips facing forward and avoid leaning forward or backward.
6. Hold the pose for a few breaths, feeling the stretch along the left side of your body.
7. Inhale and return to the center, lifting your arms overhead.
8. Exhale and repeat the pose on the left side, bending your upper body to the left and reaching your left hand towards the floor and your right hand towards the sky.

9. Hold the pose for a few breaths, feeling the stretch along the right side of your body.
10. Inhale and return to the center, lifting your arms overhead.

If you really want to increase the pose of these yoga poses, try doing them outdoors in the sun. Though I am not one to encourage sunbathing for a tan, you can also try laying in the sun while meditating and soaking up the energy of the rays. Make the most of the sun while it's out!

Because of the link between this chakra and your true self, it's also a good idea to try new things. By stepping out of your comfort zone, you get a better chance to discover your authentic self.

As you may have imagined at this point, many of the healing crystals will be yellow. You may want to keep one or some of these crystals nearby:

- Amber
- Yellow Jasper
- Yellow Topaz
- Agate
- Lemon Quartz
- Pyrite
- Citrine

Essential oils can be used but incense sticks may be more beneficial because of their relation to fire and burning. Try scents that are fiery like saffron, ginger, cinnamon, lemongrass, black pepper, and peppermint.

Ginger and turmeric are good for the solar plexus chakra. They are superfoods rich in antioxidants and can help digestion because of their anti-inflammatory properties. Try to maintain a balanced diet that has complex carbohydrates such as whole grains.

A Guided Meditation for the Solar Plexus Chakra

Begin by finding a comfortable position, either seated or lying down, and gently close your eyes. Take a deep breath in, and as you exhale, allow your body to relax and release any tension you may be holding. Feel the support of the ground beneath you, grounding you in this present moment.

Bring your attention to the area just above your navel, where your solar plexus chakra sits. Visualize a radiant, vibrant yellow light in this area, glowing with warmth and vitality. See this light expanding, filling your entire Solar Plexus, and infusing it with healing energy and balance.

Take a moment to connect with your breath. Notice the gentle rise and fall of your abdomen with each inhale and exhale. Allow your breath to deepen, inviting a sense of relaxation and ease into your body.

Now, let us explore the theme of digestion. Reflect on the incredible process that takes place within your body, transforming food into energy. Visualize the nourishing food you consume being broken down and absorbed, providing nourishment and vitality to every cell.

As you connect with this process, bring your awareness to any areas of your digestive system that may need attention. Are there any discomforts or imbalances you wish to address? Breathe into these areas, sending healing energy and love.

Imagine the golden light within your solar plexus chakra expanding and encircling your entire digestive system. See this light soothing and healing any digestive ailments or tensions, bringing balance and harmony to your gut. Feel a sense of ease and well-being washing over you.

Now, let us explore the concept of self-esteem. Reflect on how you perceive yourself and your worthiness. Are there any areas in which you struggle with self-doubt or low self-esteem? Acknowledge these feelings without judgment or criticism.

As you breathe deeply, envision the golden light within your solar plexus chakra intensifying, becoming brighter and more radiant. Feel this light expanding throughout your entire being, filling you with a profound sense of self-assurance and confidence. Embrace the understanding that you are worthy of love, success, and happiness.

Allow this newfound self-esteem to permeate every aspect of your being. Let it infuse your thoughts, your actions, and your interactions with others. Know that you are a unique and valuable individual, deserving of all the goodness life has to offer.

Now, bring your awareness to the tendency to overthink and the need to control. Notice if your mind is constantly racing, analyzing every situation, or if you find it challenging to let go and surrender. Be gentle with yourself as you observe these patterns.

Take a moment to set the intention to release the need to control and the burden of overthinking. Visualize a soft breeze flowing through your solar plexus chakra, gently clearing away any mental clutter. Feel a sense of spaciousness and calmness settling within you.

Allow yourself to surrender to the flow of life. Trust in the universe's wisdom and guidance. Know that you don't have to have all the answers or control every outcome. Embrace the freedom that comes from releasing the need to control and surrendering to the natural rhythm of life.

As you continue to breathe deeply, feel the golden light within your solar plexus chakra shining brighter than ever. Experience its warmth spreading throughout your body, revitalizing your metabolism and enhancing your energy levels. Embrace the understanding that you have the power to harness and direct this energy towards your goals and aspirations.

Take a few moments to bask in this transformative energy, allowing it to harmonize your solar plexus chakra, promoting balanced digestion, heightened self-esteem, and a release of the need to control.

Know that you possess the inner strength and wisdom to navigate life's challenges with grace and confidence. Trust in your ability to make decisions that align with your highest good and to embrace the flow of life.

When you are ready, gently bring your awareness back to your physical body. Wiggle your fingers and toes, and slowly open your eyes. Take a moment to appreciate the energy you have cultivated within your solar plexus chakra. Keep this energy with you as you calm your mind and let go of the need to control.

Affirmations for the Solar Plexus Chakra

The seed mantra to encourage balance in this chakra is *ram*. As you have worked on the previous two chakras, don't feel you only need to repeat this seed. Try repeating all three as you visualize the energy moving up through the three chakras. You can even combine the seed mantra with an affirmation.

- I am free to make my own choices
- I stand in my personal power
- I am calm, able, and confident
- I have the courage to make positive changes
- I release the need to control
- I am true to myself
- I know the right path to take
- I am worthy of my dreams
- I forgive myself for past mistakes
- I have the motivation for my ambitions

There is no one chakra that is more important than the other but considering how crucial the heart is for our emotional and physical well-being, it's a chakra that most of us need to pay more attention to.

Review Request

As an author deeply passionate about self-healing, your thoughts matter greatly to me. I kindly invite you to share your valuable review on Amazon, highlighting the strengths and insights gained from this book. Your feedback not only supports my future endeavors but also assists fellow readers in making informed choices.

Join me on this enlightening exploration of self-discovery, transformation, and empowerment. Together, let's delve into the world of chakras and the Vagus Nerve, harnessing their potential for a balanced and harmonious life.

Please click on the link if you are reading the eBook or scan the QR code if you are reading the print book to go to the review page and leave your review. I would appreciate a sentence or two but if you are busy, I would be happy with a star rating too 😊

https://www.amazon.com/review/create-review/?ie=UTF8&channel=glance-detail&asin=B0CD4G1W4H

Chapter Six:
The Heart Chakra- Anahata

Though you may think the heart chakra is over your heart, it's actually more central, in the middle of the chest, and in line with your spine. The word anahata translates to unbeaten or unstruck, which may sound ironic but the heart chakra deals with an unbeaten or infinite love. It is associated with the element of air, representing freedom and expansion.

As one would imagine, this chakra is associated with giving and receiving love, both crucial for our happiness and well-being. It's not just the love in all of our relationships but also the love that we show ourselves. This chakra has a strong connection to the circulatory system, the upper back, the thymus glands (the immune system), as well as our skin, hands, and sense of touch. With the element of air, it is also connected to our lungs.

Interestingly, ancient yogis believe that the heart chark has a frequency of 639 Hz, the frequency of love and healing. Chakras below the heart have a lower frequency as they are related to our physical selves whereas above the heart, the frequency increases as we connect to our higher selves.

The symbol for the heart chakra is a green lotus with 12 petals and two triangles inside overlapped to make a hexagon. The hexagon represents the unification of male and female energies. Each of the petals also represents qualities that can block energy.

1. Lust
2. Fraud
3. Indecision
4. Repentance
5. Hope
6. Anxiety
7. Longing
8. Impartiality
9. Arrogance
10. Incompetence
11. Discrimination
12. Defiance

Others believe that each petal represents the quality of a pure heart. These include:

1. Love
2. Harmony
3. Empathy
4. Understanding
5. Purity
6. Clarity
7. Compassion
8. Unity

9. Forgiveness
10. Kindness
11. Peace
12. Bliss

How to Recognise a Blocked Heart Chakra

Physically, you may notice heart palpitations, shortness of breath, poor circulation, frequent colds, cases of flu, and infections. When the chakra is blocked, the physical symptoms become more severe, such as high or low blood pressure, heart pain, or asthma.

Emotional symptoms of an underactive heart chakra are extensive. Again, the severity of your symptoms can indicate how underactive or even blocked the chakra is. You may feel you have low self-esteem, you are shy, or completely antisocial, to the point where you push those who care about you away. Bottling up emotions is common and this only makes them more intense. Some people will put on a tough, brave face when really, they are incredibly vulnerable. There will be struggles within relationships, perhaps with a lack of trust, a fear of rejection, a fear of commitment, or holding grudges. If you can't let go of a previous relationship, your heart chakra is probably blocked. It is even more likely to be blocked if you can't break free from a toxic relationship.

An overactive heart chakra can be seen with the need to please others to the point that you sacrifice your own needs and well-being for the benefit of others. You might be overly empathetic, too dependent on others, and it's likely that there are few healthy boundaries in your relationships.

When the heart chakra is balanced, the most powerful thing you will feel is unconditional love. If you look at the 12 qualities that are associated with the lotus petals, you get a complete understanding of what a balanced heart chakra feels like.

How to Heal the Heart Chakra and Embrace Love

Yoga, like any other physical exercise, is crucial for heart health. It can reduce stress, improve sleep, burn calories, and according to cardiologist Dr. Helene Glassberg, yoga can improve cholesterol and blood sugar levels and relax the arteries, and lower blood pressure (Penn Medicine, 2016). Here are some yoga poses that can balance the heart chakra as you work out.

Locust Pose (Salabhasana)

1. Lie down on your belly with your arms resting alongside your body, palms facing up.
2. As you inhale, lift your head, chest, arms, and legs off the ground simultaneously. Keep your gaze forward and your neck in a neutral position.
3. Engage your glutes, hamstrings, and lower back muscles to lift your legs and chest as high as possible. Press your pubic bone into the ground to lengthen your lower back.
4. Keep your shoulders relaxed and away from your ears. Reach your arms back and down towards your feet, with your palms facing down.
5. Hold the pose for 5-10 breaths, then release as you exhale.

6. Repeat the pose 2-3 times, taking breaks in between as needed.

Fish Pose (Matsyasana)

1. Lie down on your back with your legs straight out, your arms resting next to your body, and palms facing down.
2. Slide your hands under your buttocks with your palms facing down and your elbows tucked in towards your sides.
3. As you inhale, press down through your elbows and forearms and lift your chest and head off the ground. Tilt your head back and rest the crown of your head on the ground.
4. Keep your legs and feet active, pressing down through your thighs and through the tops of your feet.
5. Hold the pose for 5-10 breaths, then release as you exhale.
6. To come out of the pose, tuck your chin into your chest and slowly lower your back and head to the ground.

Tree Pose (Vrksasana)

1. Stand at the top of your mat with your feet together and your arms resting alongside your body, palms facing forward.
2. Shift your weight onto your left foot then slowly lift your right foot off the ground.
3. Place the sole of your right foot on your left inner thigh, pressing your foot into your thigh and

your thigh into your foot. Avoid placing your foot on your knee joint.

4. Find a focal point in front of you and fix your gaze on it to help maintain your balance.
5. Bring your hands together in front of your heart, palms touching. Alternatively, you can extend your arms above your head with your palms facing each other.
6. Keep your spine long and your shoulders relaxed. Engage your core muscles to help maintain your balance.
7. Hold the pose for 5-10 breaths, then release as you exhale and return to standing with your feet together.
8. Repeat the pose on the other side, balancing on your right foot and placing your left foot on your right inner thigh.

Supine Spinal Twist (Supta Matsyendrasana)

1. Lie down on your back with your legs extended and your arms resting alongside your body, palms facing down.
2. As you exhale, bend your right knee and draw it towards your chest.
3. Use your left hand to guide your right knee across your body towards the left side of your mat, keeping your right shoulder on the ground. You can also extend your right arm out to the side, palm facing up.
4. Keep your right shoulder relaxed and your gaze turned towards your right hand, or straight up towards the ceiling.

5. Hold the pose for 5-10 breaths, feeling the stretch along your spine and in your right hip.
6. Slowly release the twist as you exhale, bringing your right leg back to the center and extending it on the ground.
7. Repeat the pose on the other side, bending your left knee and drawing it towards your chest, then guiding it across your body towards the right side of your mat.

Gate Pose (Parighasana)

1. Start in a kneeling position on your mat with your legs hip-width apart.
2. Extend your right leg out to the side, keeping your foot flat on the ground and your toes pointing forward.
3. Reach your right arm up towards the ceiling and stretch your left arm out to the left, parallel to the ground, with your palm facing down.
4. As you exhale, lean your torso to the left and reach your left arm overhead, keeping your hips facing forward. You can rest your left hand on your left thigh or calf for support.
5. Keep your right arm reaching up towards the ceiling and gaze up towards your fingertips.
6. Hold the pose for 5-10 breaths, feeling the stretch along the right side of your body.
7. To come out of the pose, exhale and bring your left arm down to your side, then bring your right knee back to meet your left knee in the kneeling position.

8. Repeat the pose on the other side, extending your left leg out to the side and stretching your right arm out to the right.

Standing Backbend (Anuvittasana)

1. Stand with your feet hip-width apart, your arms resting alongside your body, and your palms facing forward.
2. Inhale and raise your arms up towards the ceiling, keeping your shoulders relaxed and your gaze forward.
3. As you exhale, lift your chest and lean back, arching your spine and bringing your hands to your lower back for support. Keep your hips and legs stable.
4. If comfortable, release your hands from your lower back and reach them towards the ground behind you. Keep your gaze up towards the ceiling or sky.
5. Hold the pose for 5-10 breaths, feeling the stretch along the front of your body and in your back.
6. To come out of the pose, inhale and slowly lift your chest back up to a neutral position, then lower your arms back down to your sides.

Half Bow (Ardha Dhanurasana)

1. Lie down on your stomach with your legs extended behind you and your arms resting alongside your body, palms facing down.
2. As you inhale, bend your right knee and reach back with your right hand to grasp your right

ankle or foot. Keep your left leg extended behind you.

3. Use your right hand to lift your right foot towards the ceiling, bringing your right knee off the ground.
4. As you exhale, lift your chest and head off the ground, reaching your left arm forward for balance.
5. Keep your right foot and hand lifting towards the ceiling, while also keeping your left leg and arm active.
6. Hold the pose for 5-10 breaths, feeling the stretch along the front of your body and in your right thigh.
7. To release the pose, exhale and slowly lower your chest, head, and right leg back down to the ground.
8. Repeat the pose on the other side, bending your left knee and reaching back with your left hand to grasp your left ankle or foot.

The heart frequency for healing and love is more based on anecdotal ancient sources but there has been some research into the effects of this frequency. It's a whole other subject but if you are interested, it is worth looking into Solfeggio Frequencies and their benefits. I have included a link for an example of the 639 Hz Solfeggio Frequency for you to listen to.

https://www.youtube.com/watch?v=5T_QxR8aclQ

The heart chakra is associated with the color green but because of the connection with love, some also relate this chakra to the color pink, especially when choosing crystals. Some of my favorite crystals for the heart chakra are:

- Rose Quartz
- Emerald
- Green jade
- Malachite
- Green Tourmaline
- Kunzite
- Green Calcite

Lavender and jasmine essential oils are associated with feminine energy whereas sandalwood and clove are associated with masculine energy. You can try creating a balance between these essential oils as they can all benefit the heart chakra. Rose is another scent with strong connections to the heart.

Leafy green vegetables and green fruits are perfect for the heart chakra as well as your overall health. Have fun experimenting with different green foods to make a smoothie or soup and try green tea as an alternative to one of your coffees.

A Guided Meditation for the Heart Chakra

Find a comfortable position and gently close your eyes. Take a deep breath in, and as you exhale, release any tension in your body, allowing yourself to fully relax. Feel the ground beneath you, helping you remain in this present moment.

Direct your attention to the center of your chest and the heart chakra, the chakra that links the lower physical chakras with the upper spiritual chakras. Visualize a radiant, emerald green light in this region, glowing with love and compassion. See this light expanding, filling your entire chest, and infusing it with healing energy and balance.

Take a moment to connect with your breath. Notice the gentle rise and fall of your chest with each inhale and exhale. Allow your breath to deepen. Notice how your body begins to relax with each breath.

Now, let's explore the theme of bottling up and suppressing emotions. Reflect on any emotions that you may have been holding back or suppressing. Are there any feelings that you find difficult to express or release? Why is it easier to push these emotions down rather than express yourself? Acknowledge these emotions without judgment or criticism. All of your emotions are there for a reason.

As you breathe deeply, envision the emerald green light within your heart chakra getting stronger, becoming brighter and more vibrant. Feel this light expanding throughout your entire body, creating a safe and nurturing space for your emotions to be acknowledged and expressed.

Imagine a gentle, soothing energy flowing into your heart chakra, melting away any barriers or blockages that hinder the free flow of emotions. See these barriers dissolving, and a sense of emotional freedom taking their place. Allow yourself to experience your emotions fully, embracing them with love and compassion.

Now, let's explore the emotions of fear of rejection and commitment. Reflect on any fears or hesitations you may have in opening your heart fully to others. Are there any past experiences that have caused you to guard your heart or fear vulnerability? Acknowledge these feelings with compassion and understanding.

Bring your awareness to the health of your physical heart. Consider the importance of a healthy heart in supporting your overall well-being. Visualize your heart beating steadily and strongly, nourishing your body with every pulse. Connect with a deep sense of gratitude for the miraculous organ that is your heart.

Take a moment to set the intention to release the fear of rejection and commitment. Visualize your heart chakra expanding, opening like a blossoming flower. Feel a sense of courage and trust emerging within you, allowing you to embrace the vulnerability and deep connections that come with opening your heart.

As you continue to breathe deeply, imagine the emerald green light within your heart chakra infusing your physical heart with healing energy. See this light surrounding your heart, strengthening and revitalizing it. Feel a sense of warmth and vitality spreading throughout your chest as your heart responds to this loving energy.

Repeat the affirmation "I am deserving of love and connection". Know that it is safe to be authentic and vulnerable, and that true strength lies in allowing your heart to guide you.

Now, let's cultivate the qualities of compassion, empathy, and forgiveness. Reflect on the interconnectedness of all beings, and the importance of treating others with kindness and understanding. Visualize a soft, warm light radiating from your heart, spreading love and compassion to everyone in your life.

Take a moment to send love and healing to any person or situation in need of forgiveness. This may include forgiving yourself or forgiving others who may have caused you pain. Breathe in forgiveness and exhale any lingering resentment or anger. Allow the healing energy of forgiveness to fill your heart, freeing you from the burdens of the past.

As you continue to breathe deeply, feel the emerald green light within your heart chakra shining brighter than ever. Experience its warmth and love spreading throughout your body and radiating out into the world. Embrace the understanding that love is your true essence, and that by opening your heart, you can create deep, meaningful connections and bring healing to yourself and others.

Take a few moments to soak up in this powerful energy, allowing it to harmonize your heart chakra, promoting emotional well-being, heart health, compassion, empathy, and forgiveness.

Know that you possess the capacity to love and be loved deeply. Trust in the wisdom of your heart and allow it to guide you in creating meaningful connections and a life filled with love.

When you are ready, gently bring your awareness back to your physical body. Wiggle your fingers and toes, and slowly open your eyes. Take a moment to appreciate the energy you have cultivated within your heart chakra and smile! Take a few more deep breaths as you imagine what you can achieve with this warming energy you now have.

Affirmations for the Heart Chakra

Yam is the seed mantra. It's pronounced in a way that combines the words ham and yum. I like to place my hand in the center of my chest as I'm chanting and imagine drawing the warmth in. Some of the following affirmations may also resonate with you.

- My heart is open to love
- I am worthy of true love
- I love and accept myself unconditionally
- I give my relationships the love they deserve
- My loved ones are free to be themselves around me
- My best is good enough
- My compassion is infinite
- I lead a happy life
- I am willing to be happy right now

Heartbreak is, unfortunately, a given part of life but for all aspects of our health, we can't afford to let it consume our lives. As our heart begins to heal, we can start looking at the throat chakra.

Chapter Seven:
The Throat Chakra- Vishuddha

The throat chakra is located at the base of your throat. The Sanskrit translation means to purify the body of harmful substances. The element associated with this chakra is space or Ether. According to Vedic philosophy, space was the first element created. The space provides us with the opportunity to increase our perspective.

The most common characteristic associated with this chakra is effective communication. The energy in this wheel enables us to speak the truth, not just with others but also with our inner selves. As well as helping us express ourselves well, this chakra can help us to find our inspiration. It is the connection between our verbal and body language. Due to its location, unhealthy food and polluted air can block this chakra but when energy is able to flow, the body detoxifies and better health is maintained.

The symbol for the throat chakra is a 16-petaled lotus. These petals represent compassion, forgiveness, self-control, calmness, pride, truthfulness, and straightforwardness, to name a few. Inside the lotus, there is an upside-down triangle with a circle in the middle, an entry point to our spiritual awareness and growth. The color blue is synonymous with communication, a pure mind free from negative thoughts, and stillness.

A balanced throat chakra will allow you to speak freely and honestly. You will be confident in your authentic self and will be open-minded. Not only this, but you will also become a better listener!

What Your Throat Chakra Is Telling You

Many of the physical symptoms are those you would expect in this part of the body. You may suffer from frequent sore throats or a raspy voice. In more severe instances, you may have laryngitis or problems with your thyroids. Mouth ulcers and gum disease affect some people. Others struggle with neck pain.

An underactive throat chakra leads to people not being able to speak up for themselves, their values, or their beliefs. While you may know what boundaries you want and need in place, you might have difficulty communicating them with others. It's possible that you can't express your feelings or you can't find the words to express them accurately. This leads you to feel that others often misunderstand you. When the thought of expressing your true feelings causes anxiety, the throat chakra could be blocked. Other signs of a blocked throat chakra include excessive use of negative words, low self-esteem, and a sense that you are conditioned by society rather than taking charge of your own future.

When the throat chakra is overactive, you may catch yourself interrupting others, talking too much and not letting others get a word in edgeways, and even gossiping!

What You Can Do for Your Throat Chakra

You may not associate yoga with the throat but a focus on deep breathing as you stretch can release tension and draw energy to your thyroids. Deep breathing is a way for me to release built-up negativity and of course, fill my lungs with clean, fresh oxygen!

Supported Shoulderstand Pose (Salamba Sarvangasana)

1. Begin by lying flat on your back with your arms along your sides, and palms facing down.
2. Bend your knees and bring your feet close to your buttocks, with your feet hip-width apart.
3. Place your hands on your lower back and gently lift your legs up towards the ceiling.
4. Press your hands into your lower back to lift your hips off the ground.
5. Bring your hands to your mid-back, supporting your spine with your palms.
6. Lift your legs up towards the ceiling and keep your body in a straight line.
7. Keep your chin tucked and gaze towards your chest to avoid straining your neck.
8. Hold the pose for 30-60 seconds, breathing deeply and steadily.

9. To come out of the pose, gently lower your legs back down to the ground, one at a time.

Plow Pose (Halasana)

1. Begin by lying flat on your back with your arms alongside your body and palms facing down.
2. Inhale and lift your legs up towards the ceiling.
3. Exhale and slowly lower your legs behind your head, bending at the waist.
4. Keep your legs straight and your toes pointed towards the ground.
5. Rest your hands on your lower back, supporting your spine with your palms.
6. Hold the pose for 30-60 seconds, breathing deeply and steadily.
7. To come out of the pose, exhale and slowly roll your spine back down to the ground, one vertebra at a time.

Tabletop Pose (Bharmanasana)

1. Begin on your hands and knees. Your wrists need to be directly under your shoulders and your knees directly under your hips.
2. Spread your fingers wide and press your palms into the ground, with your fingers pointing forward.
3. Engage your core muscles and keep your spine in a neutral position.
4. Inhale and lift your chin and chest towards the ceiling, while lowering your stomach towards the ground, creating a slight arch in your back.

5. Exhale and round your spine, tucking your chin towards your chest. Draw your belly button in towards your spine.
6. Continue to move through these two movements, coordinating your breath with each movement.
7. Hold the pose for 30-60 seconds, breathing deeply and steadily.

Bridge Pose (Setubandha Sarvangasana)

1. Lie on your back with your knees bent and your feet flat on the ground. Hips should be hip-width apart.
2. Place your arms alongside your body, keeping your palms facing down.
3. Inhale and press your feet and arms into the ground, lifting your hips up towards the ceiling.
4. Keep your thighs and feet parallel and your knees directly above your ankles.
5. Clasp your hands underneath your pelvis and lengthen your arms to lift your chest towards your chin.
6. Hold the pose for 30-60 seconds, breathing deeply and steadily.
7. Exhale and slowly release your hands, rolling your spine back down to the ground one vertebra at a time.

Downward Facing Dog Pose (Adho Mukha Svanasana)

1. Begin on your hands and knees with your wrists directly under your shoulders. Keep your knees directly under your hips.

2. Spread your fingers wide and press your palms into the ground, with your fingers pointing forward.
3. Curl your toes under and lift your hips up towards the ceiling, straightening your arms and legs.
4. Keep your feet hip-width apart and your hands shoulder-width apart.
5. Press your heels towards the ground and lengthen your spine, drawing your tailbone towards the ceiling.
6. Draw your shoulder blades down and away from your ears and broaden your collarbones.
7. Hold the pose for 30-60 seconds, breathing deeply and steadily.
8. To come out of the pose, exhale and lower your knees back down to the ground.

Lion's Breath (Simha Pranayama)

1. Begin in a comfortable seated position. You can cross your legs and rest your hands on your knees if this feels natural.
2. Take a deep inhale through your nose, filling your lungs completely.
3. As you exhale, open your mouth wide, stick out your tongue, and stretch it down towards your chin.
4. Simultaneously, exhale forcefully and make a "ha" sound from the back of your throat, while widening your eyes and contracting the muscles in your face.
5. Imagine that you are breathing out all of your stress, tension, and negative energy.

6. Repeat Lion's Breath 3-5 times, taking a few normal breaths in between each round.

Neck Rolls and Neck Stretches

Though technically not a yoga pose, these two exercises are essential for releasing tension and stiffness in the neck as well as the shoulders and upper back.

Neck Stretches:

1. Begin in a comfortable seated position, with your legs crossed and your hands resting on your knees.
2. Inhale and lift your right arm towards the ceiling.
3. Exhale and place your left hand on the top of your head, gently tilting your head towards your left shoulder.
4. Hold the stretch for 5-10 breaths, feeling the stretch along the right side of your neck.
5. Release the stretch and repeat on the other side, lifting your left arm towards the ceiling and tilting your head towards your right shoulder.

Neck Rolls:

1. Begin in a comfortable seated position, with your legs crossed and your hands resting on your knees.
2. Inhale and lengthen your spine, drawing your shoulders away from your ears.
3. Exhale and drop your chin towards your chest, feeling the stretch along the back of your neck.

4. Inhale and roll your head to the right, bringing your right ear towards your right shoulder.
5. Exhale and continue to roll your head back, bringing your head towards the back of your neck.
6. Inhale and roll your head to the left, bringing your left ear towards your left shoulder.
7. Exhale and continue to roll your head forward, bringing your chin towards your chest.
8. Repeat the neck rolls 3-5 times, alternating the direction of the rolls with each repetition.

Blue is frequently associated with bringing about a sense of calm. When blue lights were installed in 71 Japanese train stations, there was a decrease in suicide rates of 84 percent (Dreher, 2018). Stronger blues are said to stimulate clear thinking whereas softer tones calm the mind. It's worth incorporating a splash of blue into your life, especially your clothes or even a blue necklace considering the placement!

On that note, you can double the effectiveness of your jewelry and accessories by choosing those with crystals that are believed to help balance the throat chakra. These include:

- Aquamarine
- Sodalite
- Angelite
- Azurite
- Blue Calcite
- Larimar
- Kyanite
- Blue Apatite

Essential oils have long been used for throat and respiratory issues including Tee tree, eucalyptus, and mint. Lemongrass is a member of the mint family and also has that fresh, zingy aroma. Frankincense may help to develop a stronger spiritual connection and rosemary is good for mental clarity.

An increase in fluids may help balance the throat chakra, especially those that soothe the throat like honey and lemon water, and herbal teas. Try adding a handful of blueberries and blackberries to natural yogurt too!

A Guided Meditation for the Throat Chakra

Find a comfortable position and gently close your eyes. Take a deep breath in, and as you exhale relax into your position and release any built-up tension in your body. Imagine your root chakra grounded and visualize the energy freely flowing up through the chakras.

Move your attention to your throat. Visualize a vibrant, shimmering blue light in this region, radiating with clarity and truth. Watch as this light grows so that it fills your whole neck area and infuses it with healing energy and balance.

Bring your attention back to your breath as you inhale and exhale. Notice the gentle flow of air, allowing your sense of smell to take in all the scents around you. Allow your breath to deepen, inviting a sense of relaxation and calmness into your body.

Now, let's look into the theme of communicating the truth. Reflect on the power and importance of honest and authentic expression. Think about any moments in your life where you may have been withholding your truth or not speaking up for what you believe in. Be kind to yourself and don't judge yourself for these moments.

As you breathe deeply, envision the blue light within your throat chakra intensifying, becoming brighter and more vigorous. Feel this light expanding throughout your entire being, empowering your voice and your ability to communicate your truth.

Imagine this radiant blue light dissolving any fears or insecurities that may have prevented you from expressing yourself freely. Feel a sense of confidence and empowerment growing within you, allowing your voice to resonate with honesty and clarity.

Now, bring your awareness to the concept of self-expression. Reflect on the unique gifts, talents, and ideas that you possess. Embrace the understanding that your voice matters and that you have a valuable perspective to share with the world.

Take a moment to set the intention to express yourself authentically and without reservation. Visualize the blue light within your throat chakra expanding, creating a spacious and nurturing environment for your self-expression. Feel a sense of freedom and liberation as you allow your true self to shine through your words and actions.

Embrace the understanding that your authenticity is a gift to the world. By sharing your true self, you inspire and empower others to do the same. Let go of the need to apologize for who you are.

Now, let's cultivate the quality of open-mindedness. Reflect on the importance of listening to different perspectives and being open to new ideas. Acknowledge any tendencies you may have to be closed off or rigid in your thinking. Don't dwell on them, with each exhale, let these thoughts pass.

Take a moment to set the intention to cultivate open-mindedness. Visualize the blue light within your throat chakra expanding further, creating a space of openness and curiosity. Feel a sense of receptivity and willingness to consider new viewpoints and ideas.

Embrace the understanding that true growth and understanding come from embracing diverse perspectives and being open to learning from others. Allow yourself to release any preconceived notions or judgments, creating space for new insights and wisdom to enter your life.

Now, let's explore the concept of active listening. Ask yourself if you can honestly say that you listen to others completely when they are talking. Reflect on why truly hearing and understanding others when they speak is essential. Notice any tendencies you may have to interrupt or form judgments while listening.

As you continue to breathe, make a commitment to becoming an active listener. Visualize the blue light within your throat chakra expanding even further, creating a space of deep presence and attentiveness. Feel a sense of empathy and compassion as you listen to others with an open heart and mind.

Embrace the understanding that when you actively listen to others, you create a safe and supportive space for them to express themselves authentically. Through active listening, you foster connection, understanding, and harmony in your relationships.

Still keeping a focus on breathing deeply, feel the blue light within your throat chakra shining brighter than ever. Experience its clarity and truth resonating throughout your entire being. Embrace the understanding that by speaking your truth, expressing yourself authentically, cultivating open-mindedness, and engaging in active listening, you create harmony within yourself and in your interactions with others.

For the next few moments, enjoy this blue energy you have created and allow it to harmonize your throat chakra, promoting clear and authentic communication, self-expression, open-mindedness, and active listening.

Know that you possess the power to express yourself authentically and to listen with empathy and understanding. Trust in the wisdom of your voice and embrace the beauty of true and heartfelt communication.

When you are ready, gently bring your awareness back to your physical body. Wiggle your fingers and toes, and slowly open your eyes. Take a moment to appreciate and nourish your communication, self-expression, open-mindedness, and active listening. Remember your intentions and use your new energy to fulfil your communication intentions.

Affirmations for the Throat Chakra

Don't forget that singing and humming stimulate the vagus nerve and considering the vagus nerve passes the vocal cords and throat, the seed mantra *ham* (pronounced hum) can bring about some wonderful changes. For English affirmations, the focus will be on the freedom to express your true self.

- I hear and speak the truth
- I communicate with authenticity
- My voice is necessary and heard
- My words are beneficial to others
- I actively listen to my inner voice
- Gossip does not serve me
- I express my emotions fearlessly
- I have integrity
- I have the courage to stand up for myself

Remember for affirmations to truly work, you need to believe them. This is why it's important to work on each chakra in order. It's counterproductive to work on communicating your emotions if your heart chakra is imbalanced and you are lacking emotional awareness. Keeping this in mind, we are now ready to move on to the third eye chakra.

Chapter Eight:
The Third Eye Chakra- Ajna

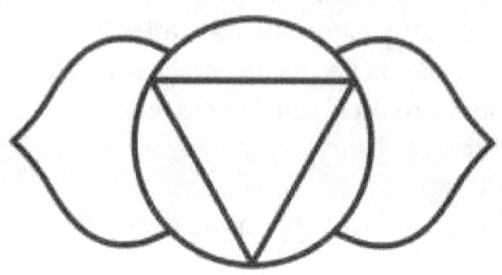

The third eye chakra isn't right between your eyes but a fraction higher on the brow. Ajna means beyond wisdom, perception, or command. There is a deep connection between spirituality and feminine energy. It is associated with the element of light. The chakra is connected with the pineal gland, which is responsible for the hormones serotonin and melatonin, a crucial part of our sleep patterns, linking this to light, day, and night.

Traditionally, the third eye chakra has been regarded as the "eye of the consciousness" whereas the throat is the first access to the consciousness. Imagine this chakra as the center of your wisdom, intuition, and self-awareness. The third eye chakra is the last of the chakras on the physical body and it governs our imagination and creative dreaming, it provides us with a visionary perspective and helps us to concrete our reality depending on what we choose to see in the world. Breaking free from black-and-white thinking and listening to our inner guidance enables greater trust in our own inner voice.

The lotus with two petals has a downward-facing triangle in the middle and is indigo. The petals represent ida, the energies of the moon, and pringala, the energies of the sun. These energy channels begin at the root chakra and snake their way up to the nostrils. The triangle inside represents enlightenment.

How to Know When the Third Eye Chakra Is Unbalanced

Physically, you may notice tension headaches, especially around the brow. Your eyesight may not be at its best or there are health issues with your vision. You may suffer from sinus problems, migraines, dizziness, or neurological disorders.

An underactive third eye chakra can lead to a lack of imagination and difficulty setting goals or making plans. It often comes with a fixed mindset, one where you believe your intelligence and abilities can't be improved. You may be in denial over certain aspects of your life. A blocked chakra can make you feel like you are stuck in a rut and you can't see your purpose in life. You know something isn't right but you can't put your finger on what it is. There could be a blanket of pessimism weighing you down and rather than embracing your spirituality, you reject it. If this chakra is overactive, you may find it hard to concentrate and suffer from nightmares, paranoia, or hallucinations.

Your memory and recall will be strong when the third eye chakra is balanced and this includes remembering your dreams. You will have greater intuition, awareness, and optimism. You will feel more decisive and overall, there will be a sense of bliss and excitement.

Balancing Your Third Eye Chakra

Aside from yoga, meditation can help unblock the third eye chakra. Meditation is not a skill we are all naturally born with, so we will begin with the steps on how to meditate and don't feel you need to begin with long periods of time. Try just a few minutes to start with.

Meditation

1. Find a quiet and comfortable space where you won't be disturbed. You can sit on a cushion, chair, or meditation bench, or you can lie down if that's more comfortable for you.
2. Set a timer for a few minutes to start with, and gradually increase the time as you become more comfortable with the practice.
3. Close your eyes, if this feels natural, and take a few deep breaths. Allow your body and mind to relax.
4. Focus your attention on your breath, noticing the sensation of the air moving in and out of your body. You can count your breaths if that helps you to stay focused.
5. When your mind starts to wander (and it will), gently bring your attention back to your breath without judging yourself. Simply observe the thoughts as they come and go, without getting caught up in them.

6. If you're finding it difficult to stay focused on your breath, you can try using a mantra, visualization, or other meditation technique to help you stay present.
7. When your timer goes off, take a few deep breaths and slowly open your eyes. Take a moment to notice how you feel, without judging or analyzing the experience.

Legs Up the Wall (Viparita Karani)

1. Begin by finding a clear wall space. Sit sideways with your right side against the wall.
2. Lie down on your back and swing your legs up the wall, keeping your buttocks close to the wall.
3. Adjust your position so that your legs are straight up the wall and your heels are resting on the wall.
4. Your arms can be by your sides or stretched out to the sides with your palms facing up, whichever is most comfortable for you.
5. Close your eyes and breathe deeply, relaxing your entire body.
6. Hold the pose for 5-15 minutes, or as long as you like.
7. To come out of the pose, bend your knees and roll onto your side, staying there for a few breaths before slowly sitting up.

Eagle Pose (Garudasana)

1. Begin standing in Tadasana (Mountain Pose), with your feet hip-width apart and your arms by your sides.

2. Bend your knees slightly and lift your left foot off the ground, crossing your left thigh over your right thigh. If possible, hook your left foot behind your right calf.
3. Extend your arms in front of you at shoulder height, parallel to the floor.
4. Cross your right arm over your left arm at the elbow, then bend both elbows and bring your palms together, fingers pointing towards the ceiling.
5. Lift your elbows and stretch your fingertips towards the ceiling.
6. Keep your gaze focused on a point in front of you and hold the pose for 5-10 deep breaths.
7. To release the pose, slowly unwind your arms and legs and return to Tadasana.
8. Repeat on the other side, crossing your right thigh over your left thigh and crossing your left arm over your right arm.

Lotus Pose (Padmasana)

1. Begin seated on the floor with your legs straight out in front of you.
2. Bend your right knee and place your right foot on top of your left thigh, as close to your hip crease as possible. Your right knee should rest on the floor.
3. Bend your left knee and place your left foot on top of your right thigh, as close to your hip crease as possible. Your left knee should rest on the floor.

4. Place your hands on your knees, with your palms facing up, and your index finger and thumb touching (in chin mudra).
5. Lengthen your spine and relax your shoulders, keeping your head and neck aligned with your spine.
6. Close your eyes and breathe deeply, focusing on your breath and allowing your body to relax.
7. Hold the pose for 1-5 minutes, or as long as you like.
8. To release the pose, slowly bring your legs back to a seated position with your legs extended in front of you.

Humble Warrior (Baddha Virabhadrasana)

1. Begin in a wide-legged stance with your feet about 3-4 feet apart and your toes pointing forward.
2. Turn your right foot out 90 degrees and pivot your left foot slightly inward.
3. Bend your right knee, keeping it directly over your ankle, and lift your arms up overhead, bringing your palms together.
4. Interlace your fingers, releasing your index finger, and point your thumbs up toward the ceiling.
5. Exhale and fold forward over your right thigh, keeping your arms overhead and your palms together.
6. Release your hands and bring your left shoulder inside your right knee, bringing your right hand to your lower back or right hip.

7. Bring your left hand behind your back and clasp your hands, stretching your arms straight and drawing your right shoulder blade onto your back.
8. Hold the pose for 3-5 deep breaths.
9. To release the pose, inhale and lift your torso up, returning to a standing position with your feet parallel.
10. Repeat on the other side, turning your left foot out 90 degrees and bending your left knee.

Candle Gazing (Trataka)

1. Find a quiet, dark room where you won't be disturbed. Sit in a comfortable position with your spine straight.
2. Place a candle on a table or surface about an arm's length away from you.
3. Light the candle and focus on the flame. Try to keep your gaze steady and focused.
4. Focus your attention on the flame and try to keep your mind from wandering. If your mind does start to wander, gently bring your attention back to the flame.
5. Continue gazing at the flame for 5-10 minutes, or as long as you like.
6. To end the practice, gently close your eyes and take a few deep breaths. Take a moment to enjoy a relaxed body and mind.

Alternate Nostril Breathing (Nadi Shodhana Pranayama)

1. Find a quiet place and sit comfortably. Keep your spine straight and your shoulders relaxed.
2. Use your right hand to form the "Vishnu mudra." This involves folding the index and middle finger of your right hand towards the palm. Place your thumb on your right nostril and your ring finger on your left nostril.
3. Close your right nostril with your thumb and inhale slowly and deeply through your left nostril. Fill your lungs with air.
4. When you reach the top of your inhalation, close your left nostril with your ring finger and release your thumb from your right nostril.
5. Exhale slowly all the way out through your right nostril.
6. Inhale slowly through your right nostril until your lungs are full.
7. When you reach the top of your inhalation, close your right nostril with your thumb and release your left nostril.
8. Exhale slowly through your left nostril.
9. This is one complete round of alternate nostril breathing. Continue for 5-10 rounds, or as long as you like.
10. To end the practice, release your hand and sit quietly for a few moments, noticing the effects of the practice on your body and mind.

Because of the association with light, try to reduce the amount of artificial light and increase the amount of natural light you are exposed to. This is more so at night. Our electronic devices emit a blue light that negatively impacts our melatonin levels and therefore sleep.

Before looking at crystals that are predominately purple and indigo, it's worth adding Black Obsidian to your list. This is a good all-around crystal, stabilizing the root chakra, bringing energy to the solar plexus chakra and wisdom to the third eye chakra. It may also help to remove toxic and negative vibes from your life. Other crystals for this chakra include:

- Amethyst
- Lolite
- Lepidolite
- Purple Fluorite
- Labradorite
- Arfvedsonite
- Celestine
- Dumortierite

For your essential oils, you can try adding bay laurel, clary sage, Juniper berry, or cypress to your diffuser, baths, or if you wish to combine activities, try using a scented candle for candle gazing.

Dark chocolate, nuts, and omega-3 (fatty acids found in salmon for example) have been linked to brain function and memory, so this is an ideal time to treat yourself to some home-baked goodies. Other foods that can increase the energy of the third eye chakra are purple foods such as grapes, eggplant, purple cabbage, purple sweet potato, and even purple carrots!

A Guided Meditation for the Third Eye Chakra

Begin by getting comfortable and gently closing your eyes. Begin with a deep breath as you concentrate on the root chakra and another deep breath for each chakra as you visualize your energy moving its way through the energy wheels towards the center of your brow. Remain grounded in this present moment.

Direct your attention to the space between your eyebrows, where your third eye chakra resides. Visualize a deep indigo light in this region, glowing with intuition and wisdom. See this light expanding, filling your entire forehead as you begin to feel a greater sense of balance.

Take a moment to connect with your breath. Allow your breath to deepen, inviting a sense of relaxation and stillness into your body as you fall into a rhythm. When you feel your lungs are full, inhale that little bit more and feel the breath open up your chest further.

Now, let's explore the theme of imagination and creativity. Reflect on the infinite possibilities that lie within your imagination. Embrace the understanding that you are a creative person, capable of manifesting your dreams and desires.

As you breathe deeply, envision the indigo light within your third eye chakra coming more intense and brighter. Think about your connection with the color and how it makes you feel. Picture this light expanding throughout across your brow, making its way through your entire body with each breath, awakening your creative potential and igniting your imagination.

Imagine this radiant indigo light stimulating your mind, unlocking new ideas, and sparking innovative thoughts. Feel a sense of inspiration and curiosity growing within you, as you tap into the limitless source of creativity within you.

Now, bring your awareness to the concept of a growth mindset. Reflect on the importance of embracing challenges, learning from setbacks, and continuously expanding your knowledge and understanding. Consider any times you may have to shied away from growth or to been fixed in your thinking. Let these experiences pass you as you recognize that you have all it takes to grow.

Take a moment to set the intention to cultivate a growth mindset. Visualize the indigo light within your third eye chakra expanding, creating a space of openness and receptivity. Feel a sense of curiosity and enthusiasm as you welcome new opportunities for expansion into your life.

Embrace the understanding that every experience holds the potential for growth and learning. Embrace challenges as stepping stones on your journey and approach them with resilience and a willingness to learn and evolve.

Now, let's explore the concept of concentration and focus. Reflect on the power of a focused mind and the ability to direct your attention towards your goals and aspirations. Notice any tendencies you may have to become easily distracted or scattered in your thinking.

Take a moment to set the intention to cultivate concentration and focus. Visualize the indigo light within your third eye chakra becoming even more radiant and intense. Feel a sense of clarity and sharpness as your mind becomes fully present and engaged.

Embrace the understanding that by cultivating concentration, you enhance your ability to bring your ideas and visions into reality. Allow yourself to become fully absorbed in the present moment, immersing yourself in the task at hand and channeling your energy towards your goals.

Now, we will explore the concept of spirituality. Reflect on your connection to something greater than yourself, whether it be a higher power, the universe, or your own inner wisdom. Acknowledge the significance of nurturing your spiritual well-being.

Take a moment to set the intention to deepen your spiritual connection. Visualize the indigo light within your third eye chakra expanding, creating a bridge between the physical and the spiritual realms. Feel a sense of peace and serenity as you align with the wisdom and guidance of your higher self.

Embrace the understanding that spirituality is a personal journey, and there are many paths to explore. Allow yourself to connect with practices or beliefs that resonate with your soul, nurturing your spiritual growth, and deepening your connection to the divine.

Now, let's address any potential tension headaches. Reflect on any areas of tension or discomfort in your head and temples. Notice if you are holding any stress or tension in this area. Acknowledge any discomfort with compassion and understanding.

Take a moment to set the intention to release tension and alleviate headaches. Visualize this light within your third eye chakra radiating healing energy to your head and temples. Feel a sense of relaxation and relief as the tension melts away, leaving you feeling calm and at ease.

Embrace the understanding that your mind and body are interconnected, and by nurturing your mental and spiritual well-being, you support your physical well-being as well.

As you continue to breathe deeply, feel the indigo light shining brighter than ever. Experience its wisdom and intuition resonating throughout your entire being. Embrace the understanding that by inviting imagination, cultivating a growth mindset, fostering concentration, deepening your spirituality, and releasing tension, you expand your consciousness and tap into your inner wisdom.

Sit with this tranquility and energy in your third eye chakra, promoting clarity, intuition, creativity, growth, and spiritual connection.

Know that you possess the ability to tap into your inner wisdom, access your creative potential, and navigate life with clarity and intuition. Trust in the guidance of your third eye and embrace the beauty of your expanded consciousness.

When you are ready, gently bring your awareness back to your physical body. Wiggle your fingers and toes, and slowly open your eyes. Take a moment to appreciate the energy you have cultivated within your third eye chakra, knowing that you can return to this practice whenever you need to balance and nourish your imagination, creativity, growth mindset, concentration, spirituality, and alleviate tension headaches.

Affirmations for the Third Eye Chakra

The seed mantra for the chakra is om and in Hindu, this is the original vibration of the universe and the source of all other vibrations. In Buddhism, om is God in the form of sound. The vibrations created by this sound help to stimulate areas of the brain that are linked to our state of calm as well as the nervous system. Affirmations for third eye chakra healing include:

- I see and think clearly
- I am insightful, thoughtful, and perspective
- I am in line with my purpose
- My inner wisdom is deep and powerful
- I trust the patterns I notice in my life
- I embrace imaginative thinking and change
- My mind is clear and open to all possibilities
- I possess the answers I seek
- I have faith in the Universe's guidance
- I am mentally strong and resilient

Not everyone is the type of person that believes in blinding moments of realization or awakening and that's okay. When you start to feel changes and increased balance in your third eye chakra, it may feel like the proverbial penny has dropped and that things just seem to fall in place. You may notice you aren't fighting against the world but more in tune with it. You may have your own completely different experience depending on your own symptoms. For some, just being free from constant migraines is all the relief they need! In our final chapter, we will look at the crown chakra.

Chapter Nine:
The Crown Chakra- Sahasrara

Located on the top of our heads, the crown chakra is the connection between the supreme Self and the divine energy. Sahasrara means infinite or thousand, and when this chakra is balanced, you can experience a universal flow of energy.

The crown chakra has the ability to change who we are, our habits, and our attitudes. When the Self is ruled by the ego, there is little room for gratitude, acceptance, and compassion. However, the crown chakra can make these qualities part of the true Self, making way for a more positive outlook on life, peace, understanding, happiness, and spiritual enlightenment. To some, this may sound a little too religious, as if we are looking up to some greater being for enlightenment. If you are feeling that the concept of the crown chakra is a little too out there for you, imagine it as a connection to your higher self, something that is more than just your physical body.

The chakra is represented by a violet (though this chakra is also associated with the color white) lotus flower with 1,000 petals. These petals symbolize the power of kundalini energy. When kundalini energy moves to the top of the brain, where all the energies meet, there is an endless amount of healing power. The circle represents infinite space for which the energy will merge into.

What to Expect When the Crown Chakra Is Unbalanced

Overall health may suffer when there is an imbalance in the crown chakra. Stress will get to you far more than it should and those tension headaches may become chronic. You may feel completely exhausted and your coordination may suffer because of this.

Many of the challenges faced with an imbalance in the crown chakra are related to your outlook on life. It is hard to connect to anything more than what our senses tell us. There may be a greater attachment to material goods to the point of becoming selfish. This is because we can't see beyond what is in front of us. Faith is often associated with religion but it is also the complete trust we have in someone or something. A blocked crown chakra causes a lack of faith as you feel yourself becoming more cynical. When too much energy flows to this chakra, you may experience apathy and/or sensitivity to light.

A balanced crown chakra makes you the master of your own mind and mental capabilities. You can understand the deeper truths about yourself. You will be more attuned to your energies and have enough energy to break through any barriers that previously held you back. Grounded, you will have a strong sense of belonging in the world.

How to Awaken Your Crown Chakra

Meditation, visualization, and breathing exercises will help you to bring your attention to your crown chakra. To gain balance here, there are some yoga practices to incorporate into your daily life:

Rabbit Stand (Sasangasana)

1. Begin in a kneeling position with your hips resting on your heels and your hands resting on your thighs.
2. Inhale deeply, and as you exhale, slowly lower your forehead to the mat in front of you, tucking your chin into your chest.
3. Reach behind your back and hold onto your heels with your hands, with your fingertips pointing toward your toes.
4. Gently lift your hips and round your spine, bringing your forehead as close to your knees as possible.
5. Hold the pose for 5-10 deep breaths, feeling the stretch in your back, neck, and shoulders.
6. To release the pose, slowly lift your hips and release your hands from your heels, bringing your hands back to rest on your thighs.
7. Sit back on your heels and take a few deep breaths before moving on to your next pose.

Reclined Bound Angle Pose (Supta Baddha Konasana)

1. Begin by lying on your back on a yoga mat.

2. Bend your knees and bring the soles of your feet together. Let your knees fall out to the sides.
3. Use blocks or pillows to support your knees, placing them under your thighs if you need more support.
4. Bring your arms out to the sides with your palms facing up.
5. Close your eyes and take several deep breaths, allowing your body to relax and settle into the pose.
6. Hold the pose for at least 5-10 minutes, or as long as you feel comfortable.
7. To come out of the pose, bring your knees back together and extend your legs out in front of you.

Happy Baby Pose (Ananda Balasana)

1. Begin by lying on your back on a yoga mat.
2. Bend your knees and bring them toward your chest.
3. Hold onto the outside edges of your feet with your hands, keeping your arms on the inside of your knees.
4. Gently open your knees wider than your torso, drawing them toward your armpits.
5. Flex your feet, bringing your heels up toward the ceiling.
6. Allow your tailbone to sink down toward the mat, relaxing your lower back and hips.
7. Hold the pose for 5-10 deep breaths. Feeling the lovely stretch in your hips and inner thighs.
8. To release the pose, gently release your feet and hug your knees back toward your chest.

Kundalini Breathing (Kundalini Pranayama)

1. Sit in a comfortable cross-legged position, with your spine straight and your hands resting on your knees.
2. Take a few deep breaths, inhaling through your nose and exhaling through your mouth, to help relax your body and mind.
3. Begin the Pranayama by inhaling deeply through your nose, filling your lungs with air.
4. Hold your breath for a few seconds, and then exhale forcefully through your nose, as if blowing out a candle.
5. Repeat this breath pattern, inhaling deeply through your nose, holding your breath, and exhaling forcefully through your nose, for several rounds.
6. After several rounds, release the breath and sit quietly, allowing the energy to settle and integrate into your body.
7. To complete the practice, take a few deep breaths, and then slowly open your eyes.

Wide Angle Seated Forward Bend (Upavistha Konasana)

1. Begin by sitting on a yoga mat with your legs straight out in front of you.
2. Open your legs out to the sides as wide as you can, flexing your feet and engaging your thigh muscles.
3. Inhale deeply, lengthening your spine, and then exhale as you fold forward from your hips, keeping your spine straight.

4. Walk your hands forward on the mat, reaching as far as you can while maintaining a straight spine.
5. Keep your legs engaged and flexed as you deepen the stretch with each exhale.
6. If you can, rest your forearms on the mat in front of you, or place your hands on your ankles or shins.
7. Hold the pose for 5-10 deep breaths, feeling the stretch in your hamstrings, inner thighs, and lower back.
8. To release the pose, inhale as you slowly lift your torso back up to a seated position.

Half Headstand Pose (Ardha Sirsasana)

1. Begin by kneeling on the floor with your hands and forearms on the mat, interlacing your fingers.
2. Place the top of your head on the mat, in front of your interlaced hands, creating a tripod with your forearms and head.
3. Tuck your toes under and lift your hips up, coming into a modified Downward Dog position.
4. Walk your feet toward your head, keeping your hips high and your neck long.
5. Slowly lift one leg up toward the ceiling, bending the knee and bringing it toward your chest.
6. Once you feel balanced, slowly lift the other leg off the mat, extending it toward the ceiling.
7. Hold the pose for a few deep breaths, keeping your core engaged and your gaze at a point between your hands.

8. To release the pose, slowly lower one leg at a time back to the mat, coming back into a kneeling position.

One Legged Camel Pose (Eka Pada Ustrasana)

1. Begin in a kneeling position on your yoga mat, with your knees hip-distance apart and your hands resting on your lower back.
2. Engage your core and slowly begin to arch your back, lifting your chest up toward the ceiling and leaning back.
3. Reach back with your left hand and hold onto your left heel or ankle, lifting your left leg off the mat.
4. Keep your right hand on your lower back for support and balance.
5. If you can, slowly reach your right arm up toward the ceiling, keeping your gaze up toward your fingertips.
6. Hold the pose for several deep breaths, feeling the stretch in your chest, hips, and thighs.
7. To release the pose, slowly lower your left leg back down to the mat, bringing your hands back to your lower back.
8. Repeat the pose on the other side, holding for the same amount of time.

Never underestimate the power of silence. Many people are uncomfortable with silence as it gives the brain a chance to run away with thoughts. Even if you aren't meditating, try to enjoy some time of peace and quiet and if that's not possible, switch off anything that makes a noise and listen to the sounds of nature. Practicing gratitude can also improve the crown chakra as we are able to step away from the hustle and bustle of life and take a moment to appreciate the bigger things. I keep a gratitude jar in my kitchen, write down something I am grateful for, and pop it in the jar each day.

For those looking to increase their energy through crystals, once again purple is a good choice but so are the clear and white stones.

- Clear Quartz
- Selenite
- Howlite
- Sugilite
- White Agate
- Charoite
- White Calcite

To add to your collection of essential oils, you may want to try lavender, myrrh, rosewood, or jasmine. Ginger is a popular scent, that is if you like the strong spicy smell.

The same can be applied to food. Ginger can be added to sweet and savory dishes as well as made into a herbal tea but it's only going to improve your outlook on life if you like the flavor. For the crown chakra, try to avoid processed food as much as possible and where possible, maintain as clean a diet as possible with nutrient-rich foods.

A Guided Meditation for the Crown Chakra

Please find a quiet and comfortable space where you can relax and fully engage in this guided meditation. Close your eyes, take a deep breath, and let the worries of the outside world melt away. In this journey, we will explore the crown chakra, the energy center that connects us to higher consciousness and universal wisdom. As we delve into this meditation, we will focus on enhancing our senses, gaining a new perspective on life, cultivating faith and trust, releasing chronic stress, and awakening the powerful energy of Kunalindi. Let's begin.

Take a moment to settle into a comfortable position, allowing your body to relax completely. Feel the weight of your body sinking into the surface beneath you. Bring your attention to your breath, taking a deep inhale through your nose, and exhale through your mouth, releasing any tension or tightness.

As you continue to breathe deeply and rhythmically, envision a soft, white light descending from above, surrounding your body and illuminating your crown chakra at the top of your head. Allow this warm, radiant light to gently enter your energy center, awakening and activating your crown chakra.

Sense the energy of the crown chakra expanding and blossoming like a beautiful lotus flower. Feel each of its petals opening and imagine the vibrant violet color radiating from within. As this energy expands, it fills your entire body, bringing a deep sense of peace and tranquility.

Now, imagine yourself standing in a lush, serene meadow. Visualize the vibrant green grass beneath your feet, gently swaying in the breeze. Observe the myriad of colorful flowers blooming around you, filling the air with their delicate fragrance. Feel the warmth of the sun on your skin and the gentle touch of the wind as it brushes against your face. Take a moment to fully immerse yourself in this beautiful sensory experience, allowing your senses to awaken and come alive.

As you connect with nature's beauty, allow yourself to reflect on the grand tapestry of life. Consider the vastness of the universe and your place within it. Realize that you are a unique and integral part of the cosmic dance of existence. Recognize that just as each flower and blade of grass has its purpose and contributes to the overall harmony of nature, so too do you have a special role to play in the unfolding of the universe.

Shift your focus inward now, to the crown chakra at the top of your head. Feel its energy expanding and extending upward, reaching beyond the confines of your physical body. Sense the connection between your crown chakra and the divine, the universal consciousness that permeates all things. In this moment, know that you are a vessel for higher wisdom and divine guidance.

Allow this connection to deepen your faith and trust in the unfolding of life. Understand that everything happens for a reason and that even in challenging times, there is a greater purpose at play. Trust in the divine timing of the universe and have faith that everything is working out for your highest good. Things may come to mind that make you believe this isn't true.

Now, bring your awareness to any areas of chronic stress or tension within your body. As you exhale, release these tensions. Let the universe share your load. Imagine the stress dissolving and being replaced by a sense of deep relaxation and calm. Feel the lightness and freedom that comes from releasing these burdens.

As you continue to breathe deeply, imagine a powerful energy, known as Kunalindi, flowing down from the cosmos, through your crown chakra, and into your whole body, even the tips of your fingers and toes. This divine energy is healing, transformative, and purifying. Allow it to flow effortlessly, clearing away any remaining blockages or limitations within your crown chakra and energy system.

Feel this vibrant energy filling you with a renewed sense of purpose and vitality. It illuminates your mind, allowing you to access higher levels of consciousness and insight. Sense the expansion of your awareness and the deepening connection with the divine.

Take a few moments to bask in this divine energy, allowing it to nurture and nourish your entire being. Know that you are supported, guided, and connected to the infinite wisdom of the universe.

As we come to the end of this meditation, gently bring your awareness back to your physical body. Wiggle your fingers and toes, allowing yourself to fully return to the present moment. Take a final deep breath, and when you are ready, slowly open your eyes.

Remember, you can revisit this meditation whenever you feel the need to reconnect with your crown chakra and expand your consciousness. Trust in the process and have faith that the universe is conspiring in your favor. Embrace the power of your crown chakra and allow it to guide you on your journey of spiritual growth and self-discovery.

Affirmations for the Crown Chakra

For the seed mantra, some will chant om, others ah, and some feel that there is no mantra for this chakra, hence the silence! Whether you choose the seen mantra or not, there are still plenty of affirmations to use, such as:

- I am at one with a higher power
- My chakras are aligned and balanced
- I find the connections in my life
- I am both grounded and connected to a higher self
- I am filled with light and love
- I know deep, inner peace
- I am worthy of divine energy
- I am love and I am light
- Pure, bright light flows through me
- My higher self guides me

Keeping with the theme of this lotus, there are an infinite number of affirmations not only for the crown chakra but for all of them. Feel free to use the affirmations in this book as a starting place or change any words that don't ring true to you. You can even make up your own affirmations, or even one that balances all seven. We will end this chapter with the translation of the 7 seed mantras:

I am. I feel. I do. I love. I speak. I see. I know.

Chapter Ten: Mindfulness for the Chakras and Vagus Nerve

Take a moment to sit down and just think about all of your current worries. I'm doing the same, ok! You start off with the smaller things like what on earth you can find for dinner, that's not the same as every night. The to-do list for tomorrow. What your children have been up to and if they are alright. The mistake you made last month but can't forget. What is going to happen when the car breaks down again.

Once you have finished your list take a second moment to recognize how these concerns are about the past and the future. Where you are sat at this precise present moment isn't causing you any suffering. This is the core of mindfulness, living in the present, accepting yourself for who you are, and without judgment. It involves paying attention to your thoughts and feelings and above all, your senses.

Why Is Mindfulness so Popular Today

Mindfulness is becoming increasingly popular and important in today's world because of the increased stress we face and the greater understanding we have of how this stress impacts the body. The pandemic can't be blamed for everything but it certainly woke us all up to the pressures we have and even the distractions from what is important in life. Many of us were forced to slow down and consider our lives on a deeper level. There was no way to just get up and go to work, burying or avoiding that which distressed us, and on top of that, there was the added stress that the pandemic brought us. It was a unique time that emphasized the need for greater mental and physical care.

Mindfulness isn't something that has sprung up in the last couple of years but research into the benefits has definitely increased and the practice has even been incorporated into various therapies. For example, mindfulness-based cognitive therapy (MBCT) combines mindful-based stress reduction practices with cognitive-behavioral therapy. MBCT can be effective at treating depression and what's more, as effectively as antidepressants but without the side effects.

Mindful-based stress reduction is used to help those suffering from stress and anxiety and in as little as 8 weeks, people are able to better understand their thoughts, feelings, and behaviors, which overall, leads to better emotional regulation. If we are honest with ourselves, we could all improve how we handle our emotions at times.

Surprisingly, mindfulness can also boost our cognitive abilities. During mindful practices, we train our brains to be more focused while leaving distractions behind us. It enables us to intentionally suppress thoughts and feelings that take our attention away from the task at hand. Bear in mind, this isn't the same as permanently trying to suppress them!

Amazingly, this can help with improving our memories too. Many of our moments of forgetfulness, like forgetting where those car keys are or what you need to buy at the store are caused by something called proactive interference. This is when our old memories get in the way of us accessing the newer ones. I love the thought of this as it helps me to believe that mindfulness can help me stop reliving past mistakes and instead, access the information on what I have learned from those mistakes.

You don't have to take my word for it. A study carried out by Harvard Medical School showed that 30 minutes of daily mindfulness practices over 8 weeks physically changed the brain. MRI scans of participants showed the gray matter in the hippocampus increased. This part of the brain is associated with memory and learning. The same MRI scans showed a decrease in gray matter in the amygdala, the art of the brain that is linked to stress and anxiety (Aura, n.d.).

Where Eastern and Western Philosophies Collide

There is no doubt that mindfulness has numerous physical and psychological benefits but interestingly, the Eastern and Western philosophies take a different approach. In Buddhism, mindful meditation is an essential practice to discover the cause of suffering, removing themselves from self-centeredness and the need to fulfill one's own desires. This takes them to the path of enlightenment, wisdom, and the end of suffering. Essentially, it's a practice that puts the person into a state of no self.

When it comes to the modern Western approach, there is a lot more emphasis on the self. We often hear of words such as self-compassion, and self-acceptance. Mindfulness plays an important role in self-care too. This approach involves being kinder to the self rather than a state of mind that has no self. By regularly practicing mindfulness, we can become more self-aware and this can help manage stress levels.

I am often intrigued by these different approaches. What I love is that one practice comes from thousands of years of faith and the other has a scientific perspective. Despite these differences, mindfulness is a simple, yet powerful practice and personally, it has enhanced my own physical and mental healing as I work on balancing my chakras.

Mindful Meditation and the Vagus Nerve

Mindfulness can be practiced along with many other Eastern practices, particularly yoga and meditation. Mindful meditation is not as easy as it sounds and it's not a case of just sitting there thinking of nothing. But the good news is there are so many videos now available that guide you through the process. It gives you a voice to listen to and as silly as this sounds, a reminder to breathe deeply. When your mind starts to get distracted, guided meditation helps to pull your focus back. The more I practiced mindful meditation, the easier it became, and I was able to meditate for longer. You will notice that at the end of this chapter, there is a guided meditation that will help balance the relevant chakra. You can either listen to the audible book or record the script to help you.

Here, rather than a guided meditation, I wanted to offer some advice on how I combine mindfulness, meditation, and the vagus nerve. Rather than telling you how to do it, I think it is nice at this stage for you to explore more of what works for you based on what you have learned so far.

I like to begin with some essential oils. I'm not saying I give myself a luxurious massage but there are a few essential oils that promote relaxation and calm the vagus nerve such as peppermint, lavender, bergamot, and chamomile. I add a couple of drops to a moisturizer and treat my face, neck, and shoulders with a boost of plant nutrition, paying extra attention to long, slow strokes up and down the neck (not just for the wrinkles but remember where the vagus nerve passes!).

Whenever possible, I will try to go outside because I feel there is so much more to tingle the senses. After taking off my shoes, I will use my scented moisturizer to massage my feet. According to the teachings of traditional Thai Massage, there are vagus nerve reflexes or acupressure points on the soles of the feet. Next, I will find a grassy spot to plant my feet on. There are no awkward crossed legs or namaste hands, it's important to feel comfortable.

From here, I will take long, deep breaths where the exhale is longer than the inhale. Some days it will be 5 or 6 breaths, other days, I have time for 15 to 20. During this moment, I focus on what I can hear, see, smell, and touch. There is always a bird or two tweeting so I will focus on the sounds that go beyond that.

It won't make sense until you try it but having my bare feet on the grass literally energizes me. So that you don't think I am some Snow White hippy dancing around in the garden talking to the birds, science has also proven the benefits of bodily contact with the ground. Earthing, also known as grounding, allows you to contact Earth's natural electric charge. As we have learned, everything contains energy! Activities such as lightning strikes and solar radiation renew the Earth with subatomic particles, a natural negative electric charge. This energy has been called 'electric nutrition' and contact with grass, soil, and even stones can transfer this electric nutrition to the body. Earthing has been known to reduce pain, improve sleep, and improve vagal tone (Menigoz, et. al., 2020).

When earthing was practiced in Pennsylvania State University Children's Hospital Neonatal Intensive Care Unit, premature babies' parasympathetic tone was raised in just minutes (Peachman, 2017). I'm a sucker for all babies and for me, it warms my heart to hear how we can help babies naturally rather than machines and medication!

The next stages of my mindful meditation often depend on my mood. If I know I am feeling particularly stressed or I have a lot on my mind, I will use YouTube to play low-frequency music. If my mind is calmer, I will hum. Some days I will sit there for 5 minutes, others 20. It's about what feels right for that moment.

If I am feeling sluggish and I know my body needs more energy, I will use visualization. I imagine the energy from the earth being drawn up through my feet and passing through each of the chakras. Once this energy reaches the crown chakra, it passes back to the base of the spine and then along the vagus nerve. I imagine the energy branching out into my lungs and heart, all the way down to my stomach. If you are just starting out with grounding and visualization, it will help to start on a sunny day when the ground has had a chance to warm up.

I have heard various people tell me that meditation is not for them and even after committing to the practice with an open mind, they didn't experience the benefits. That's ok! The world would be a boring place if we were all the same. Fortunately, there are many ways to practice mindfulness.

8 Mindful Activities

For each of these activities, try to ensure that you have at least 5 minutes of peace and quiet when you don't feel rushed. Any act of pleasure should be fully enjoyed. Picking up your favorite book and losing yourself in the pages isn't the same as speed reading for 5 minutes because the dinner is burning!

Candle gazing

Candle gazing, also known as Trataka, is a form of meditation that uses an object to improve focus. The eyes are open so it is often good for beginners who struggle with mental distractions. Traditionally, this is a type of meditation that encourages spiritual advancement and brings energy to the third eye. It may help improve your focus and concentration.

Make sure the room is quite dim so that the candle flame is brighter. Choose a comfortable place to sit with the candle at eye level. Begin by gazing at the candle flame. You will notice that the background will become less predominant as you continue to focus and the same thing will happen with your thoughts. Focus on your breath and imagine the energy from the candle flowing into you as you inhale and I like to imagine negative energy and stress flowing out as I exhale.

Some like to choose a candle of a certain color for a specific intention. I like indigo because of the connection to the third eye but here are some other colors and their qualities to help you choose:

- White- purity, simplicity, completion
- Gold- prosperity, abundance, spirituality
- Violet- higher consciousness, commitment
- Blue- self-expression, trust, creativity
- Green- healing, love, compassion, forgiveness
- Yellow- self-esteem, courage, ambition
- Orange- sexual energy, happiness, friendship
- Red- strength, vitality, family connections
- Pink- empathy, loyalty

You may also want to choose a scented candle. Wherever possible, choose non-toxic candles like those made from beeswax or soy. You can even get creative and make your own!

Mindful eating

I feel like over the last few decades, our relationship with food has changed. In the past, meals were prepared from scratch and the family would sit down and eat together. With today's cost of living, both parents have to go to work and that leaves evenings in a mad rush. More people turn to convenience food not just because of the time, but also because it's cheaper. As a result of our busy schedules, meals are wolfed down, more of an additional task than a chance to fuel our bodies.

One side of mindful eating is paying more attention to what we are putting in our bodies. It's about choosing foods similar to those in the Mediterranean diet such as fresh fruits and vegetables, and wholegrains. The other side to mindful eating is about using all of your senses to fully appreciate food. It's about slowing down at mealtimes, taking smaller bites, and properly chewing food.

One of the most popular mindful eating practices is with a raisin to begin switching from the way we automatically eat our food. Take a raisin and place it in your hand. If you don't like raisins, try it with another piece of dried fruit or nut. Take a moment to look at it, the different tones and wrinkles, and notice the texture between your fingers. Close your eyes so you aren't just relying on the sense of sight. Smell the raisin. At first, you will think that raisins don't smell of anything but when you are fully engaging your senses without a wandering mind, you will notice there is a smell. Your body may also react to the smell with increased saliva or a flutter in your stomach. Put the raisin in your mouth but don't chew it yet. Pay attention to how it feels on your tongue. Then start to chew the raisin as the flavor starts to awaken the next sense. The final part is not to swallow it for the sake of it but to make a conscious decision to swallow it.

Mindful eating can be practiced with any meal or snack. Even if it's your favorite comfort food, you can benefit from eating in the present moment.

Mindful walking

Much like eating, it's something that we do every day and on autopilot. It's a task to get us from A to B and if you are anything like I was, it would be a chance to process a dozen things that were racing through my mind.

It goes without saying that the best form of mindful walking is going to be in nature and where possible, barefoot. But again like eating, it doesn't have to be reserved for special walks, it can be practiced any time you walk. I have at least five 30-minute walks a week to make sure I'm getting enough physical exercise. Most people associate mindfulness with slower movements but I start off at a normal pace and then speed up to increase my heart rate. I have found that even brisk walking can be mindful.

Begin your walk with a few intentional breaths and notice how your body is feeling, the good and the bad. For example, I often begin a walk noticing a twinge in my lower back. The trick is not to get bogged down by this pain or start to think about how it is going to affect the walk. Notice it and accept it. As you start to walk, pay close attention to the different parts of your body. What does the ground feel like beneath your feet, how are you carrying your head and shoulders? Are you noticing the twinge of pain loosens up?

After listening to your body, turn your focus to the outside. What can you hear, see, and smell? Do so without judgment. The sad fact is that not everyone has access to the fresh country air and walking in the city, the sound of cars and the smell of pollution isn't the same. Now isn't the time to have a mental rant about the state of the environment. If you find your mind wandering, forgive yourself, and bring your attention back to your breathing and your senses. When you have finished, again, don't just jump into the next activity. Take a moment to notice how your body feels.

Body scan

I love body scans just before I fall asleep because I notice the built-up tension in the body and this is a good way to release it and feel far more relaxed. For this reason, I always do it in bed as I don't want to have to move afterward and break that sense of peace and calm.

Begin by laying down with your arms by your side and you can probably guess that the first thing is a few deep breaths! There is no specific part of the body to start with but in my mind, there is something more logical about starting at your feet. Tense your feet and hold it there for a moment, then release the tension. Inhale as you tense and exhale as you release. Move up to your calves, tense, and release as you breathe. Repeat the same all the way up through your body. Most people associate tension in the body up to their neck and shoulders but don't forget all those muscles in your face.

Once you have finished, keep taking those deep breaths. If you are one of the unlucky ones who take forever to fall asleep, it may surprise you how easily you drift off after a body scan.

Mindful coloring

This is a wonderful activity that lets you get in touch with your inner child. Have you ever watched a young child color? They are experts at blocking everything else out and focusing solely on their picture. As a parent trying to get their attention it might be frustrating but if you put yourself in their shoes, it's inspiring. On that note, if you have children, ask if you can join in with them. They will revel in this quality time together!

It doesn't matter what you color. You might want to draw your own doodle, print off an image, or treat yourself to an adult coloring book. Mandalas appeal to me not just because of their history with Buddhism but also because I find order in the geometric shapes.

Mindful coloring goes deeper than choosing certain colors. It's about noticing how the pencil (pen, paintbrush, chalk, etc.) feels in your hand and the smell of the materials. It's always nice to have a couple of different materials to explore the different feelings on paper and even the different sounds these materials make.

The beauty of coloring is that there is no right or wrong way to do it. You can choose any colors, any patterns, and start at any point. If you aren't feeling creative, begin with shades of blue and go from there.

The Pomodoro Technique

Many will wonder what a time management tool is doing as part of a mindful exercise but I discovered that this helps me to make mindfulness part of my daily routine. This is a very simple technique where you set a timer and work for 25 minutes and then have a 5-minute break, completing one Pomodoro. After several Pomodoros, you can take a longer break of 20 or 30 minutes.

Using this technique makes better use of your time and reduces the urge to multitask. Knowing that a break is coming up, the 25 minutes of work are more intense and productive. The 5-minute break gives you a chance to step away from work, have a stretch, do a yoga pose, breathe deeply, or do any other mindful practice you feel like doing.

Another advantage of better time management is that getting more done in shorter periods of time allows you to take part in longer activities like going for walks, enjoying a guided meditation, or having the time to appreciate your meal!

Mindful cleaning

"Please, mindful cleaning!" I hear you say. Yes, even cleaning can be more mindful. It's a necessary evil that occupies some time of each of our days and considering it can't be ignored, it's best to find a way to get the most out of it. Here are my top tips for mindful cleaning:

- If you have children, send them off with your partner or someone else you trust. If you have a partner...send them off!
- Remove any distractions, hide your phone so you aren't tempted to spend your free time on social media.
- Put your favorite music on and notice how this immediately changes your mood.
- When washing dishes, take time to focus on the temperature of the water, how the bubbles feel on your hands, and tune your breathing into the repetitive motion as you clean.
- When dusting or sweeping, notice the tiny particles as you clear an area. Watch how the

dust leaves the surface and clings to the cloth or how it settles into a dustpan.
- Use mopping as a chance to focus on the repetition of your movements and the sparkle in the floor.
- Fold laundry and take in the smell of the freshness, the colors of the clothes and the feeling of different fabrics.
- Feel the weight of the iron in your hands and focus on how your arms and shoulders feel as you watch the creases melt away.
- Don't rush the process. Use both hands and treat the task as an opportunity to improve your well-being rather than a chore that must be done.
- When you have finished, take a moment to look around and be grateful for the home you have.

Mindful cleaning doesn't just apply to your home. The next time you take a bath or a shower, do so with intention. Calm the mind of the chatter and focus on what your senses are telling you.

Engaging the senses

Our final, simple mindful exercise can be done anywhere and at anytime and I try to take advantage of those moments where you can't do anything else productive, like picking up children or waiting in queues.

Start by looking around and find 5 things you can see. Don't just list them, look at them for details. Next, find 4 things you can touch. You don't necessarily need to touch them, you can imagine what they would feel like. After touch, comes 3 things you can hear followed by 2 things you can smell. Finally, and this may be the hardest, but one thing you can taste.

This is also an excellent technique to help ground you in times of stress and anxiety. Instead of letting thoughts and feelings take over, calm the vagus nerve with some deep breaths and begin this activity.

Whether being in the present or trying to calm yourself down, this practice will be more effective if you focus on the smallest detail. It's easy to spot a car, a plant, etc. It requires more focus to purposefully focus on a crack in the wall.

In our final chapter, we are going to tie all of our learning together with a practical plan to maintain balanced chakras with daily habits that will turn into a great routine.

Chapter Eleven:
A Week of Practices to Maintain Balanced Chakras

Let's imagine chakra healing similar to a diet. You have kept to your diet for the set number of weeks and you have lost the weight you had intended to. The objective has been reached. But then after a few weeks, the weight creeps back on. You can follow each of the healing techniques in the chapter and marvel at the difference but in order not to revert back to past problems, it's necessary to continue to keep your chakras flowing with energy.

There are two ways to create a weekly plan. The first is to practice chakra-specific techniques on days that relate to that chakra because you can tune into the planetary energies. Here is what this would look like:

- The root chakra- Saturday because of the link to Saturn, the planet of karma and time, representing vigor, self-discipline, and protection. Saturn is associated with limitations and along with karma, can teach us valuable lessons for personal development.
- The sacral chakra- Monday or moon day. The moon represents feminine energy and fertility. You can also take advantage of Friday as Venus rules over this day. Not only is Venus feminine energy but it is also associated with sex and sensuality.
- The solar plexus chakra- Tuesday and the planet Mars and masculine energy. This day is associated with willpower, determination,

productivity, and courage. Sunday is sometimes used as a healing day because of the solar energy from the Sun.
- The heart chakra- Wednesday and the planet Mercury and its link to communication. The heart has a unique form of communicating information to the brain. Naturally, Friday and the planet Venus can help with heart-related healing.
- The throat chakra- Thursday and the planet Jupiter. Jupiter is connected to travel and growing energies as well as good fortune and communication. Chakra work can also be performed on Wednesday because of the ties to communication.
- The third eye chakra- Monday, Thursday, or Friday. Monday because of the relationship with the Moon and its ties to the subconscious. You can practice on Thursday because of Jupiter's connection to expansion and higher wisdom and Friday as Venus is the planetary ruler of this chakra.
- The crown chakra- Sunday is an ideal day because of its association with the Sun. The sun is the provider of our heat and light, energizing us as well as enabling our food to grow. There is also a powerful connection to enlightenment and higher consciousness as the sun can provide spiritual nourishment from divine light.

For the busy person, this might be a lot to remember, so an alternative is to work with the first chakra on Mondays and each of the following days to work your way up the spine. Again, please don't feel that this is a strict outline but rather an inspiration. You can create your own structure by taking strategies from each chapter to use on certain days or mix and match a little of all. It's always going to be what feels right for you. In this weekly plan, I have combined research into the planets and their energies on days of the week and my own personal experiences. I highly recommend starting each day with a few of the yoga poses we covered in each chapter.

Because there are lots of elements that play a role in our healing, I have included a brief review of my intentions for each day.

Monday

The Moon/ Sacral Chakra/ Root Chakra/ Red

Few people, myself included, like Monday mornings and the harsh start to the working week. Try to set your alarm a little earlier in order to plan the next 5 days. Check your calendar for any extra meetings or appointments and spend a few moments thinking about what makes you feel safe in the world.

When getting dressed, try to incorporate red for the root chakra. The color silver is often associated with the Moon and Monday. If you aren't keen on silver clothes, opt for jewelry instead. As the moon is pale white, this is another good color for Mondays but not to be used excessively. Something as simple as a white pearl or Mother of Pearl on a silver chain may help.

In Veda, moonstone is said to be made of solidified moonbeams and the ancient Greeks and Romans thought it was made from the light of the Moon. Selenite is another good choice, named after the ancient Greek Goddess of the Moon. If you already have Lapis Lazuli, keep it with you on a Monday. This 'Stone of Heaven' looks like the night sky. For aromatherapy, stick to earthy scents as well as yarrow or geranium, oils of the Moon.

While working on the root chakra on Mondays, you can boost your happy hormones and increase the feeling of being grounded by dancing as this literally keeps your feet on the ground.

My favorite recipe for a Monday is carrot and beetroot soup as you have two root vegetables and a rich red color of the beets. To make the soup, I use 1 ½ cups of cubed beetroot, 1 carrot, and 2 cups of water per person. I will also add garlic, fresh ginger, onions, a tomato, and salt and pepper but the amount is up to your taste buds. After frying the onion, ginger, and garlic in a little olive oil, I add all of the ingredients and bring to the boil. Once the root vegetables are soft, use a stick blender to make the soup.

If you are still awake when the moon is out, try meditating under the moonlight or using the Moon for gazing meditation instead of a candle.

Tuesday

Mars/ Solar Plexus Chakra/ Sacral Chakra/ Orange

As orange is associated with happiness, begin your Tuesday by doing something you enjoy rather than jumping straight into your routine. A glass of fresh orange juice will also boost your energy levels.

Mars represents our willpower, determination, and effectiveness and this is a great day to tackle a challenge. We can appreciate the active masculine energy of Mars to help us achieve these tasks. Aside from bringing a little orange to your day, take advantage of the solar plexus chakra and yellow. And because of the location of these chakras and the link with sexuality, it wouldn't hurt to wear something that awakens your sensual side.

In astrology, Mars has malefic effects such as impulsiveness, a short temper, and abuse. Wearing red coral can reverse these malefic effects because the gemstone is known for protecting Mars. To connect with the fiery energy of Mars, choose crystals that match this power, such as Red Jasper. Ginger, basil, black pepper, and cinnamon are associated with Mars and fortunately, all can be used in aromatherapy and cooking.

For a tasty orange dinner for the sacral chakra, you can try orange tofu stir fry. The trick is to use extra firm tofu that you press well to remove any excess liquid. This takes around 15 minutes so in the meantime, mix some cooking oil with 1/ cup of orange juice and the zest of one orange with some honey and garlic, salt, and pepper. Take one spoonful of the mixture to sauté the tofu. Remove the cooked tofu. With the rest of the mixture, sauté your favorite vegetables, then add the tofu back to the pan and mix.

During the day, spend a few minutes thinking about your goals and your desires and what the next steps could be to achieve them.

Wednesday

Mercury/ Heart Chakra/ Solar Plexus Chakra/ Green

It's Hump Wednesday! If your week has been going well, it's a good sign that it will keep going this way. If your week hasn't had the best start, today is a good turning point. Start your day with a positive affirmation that fills you with confidence and good feelings.

The planet Mercury is linked to nature and the environment. It makes sense that it's represented by green, much like the heart chakra. Have your morning coffee in your garden or at least look out of a window with natural views. If that's not possible, even looking at images of nature has been shown to boost the mood.

The 'communicator' planet helps us to get things done with speed and agility. To tap into the planet's power, use the crystal cinnabar which is made of mercury. Another mercury crystal is Blue Agate, a quartz mineral that can bring you confidence and calmness. Finally, Peach Aventurine is another mercury crystal that balances the yin and yang, which I like to associate with the heart chakra and the connection with the body and mind. Mercury is associated with lavender, lemongrass, peppermint, and eucalyptus.

For a Wednesday healing recipe, I combine yellow and green in a curry! Start by frying some chopped onion in a little oil, adding turmeric, ginger, and curry powder (or a paste if you have one). Once the onions are soft, add chopped garlic and then diced chicken breasts. Stir this well before adding coconut milk. At this point, I add salt and pepper followed by a quick taste in case I need any more of the powders for more heat. You can add a splash of lime juice and a teaspoon of brown sugar if you like. If not, add shredded spinach and chopped cilantro 5 minutes before serving.

Time in the sun will help you absorb a little more yellow into your life. But that's not always possible. Instead, take one of your (clean) yellow crystals and add it to a glass of water to make a crystal elixir. Leave the crystal in the water for 30 minutes before removing it and then drinking the water.

Thursday

Jupiter/Heart Chakra/Throat Chakra/ Yellow-Blue

Some people associate Jupiter with yellow and strong blue rays, others associate it with the color blue. In both cases, we can tie this to the throat chakra and as blue is such a calming color, you can wear this color on Thursday to help you get one step closer to the weekend or any day when you feel stress levels might be higher. Before getting dressed, you might want to try a yoga position where blood can flow toward the throat and improve communication.

Most of the crystals connected with Jupiter are yellow. For example, the Yellow Sapphire can help bring about wealth and good fortune. Yellow Topaz produces radiant energy and helps create balance. This crystal is also associated with the solar plexus chakra and the third eye chakra, so I like how it encompasses the Throat and heart chakras. Pink Topaz is linked to wealth, wisdom, and love, which is appropriate because the heart chakra is sometimes represented by the color pink.

To further tap into the power of Jupiter on a Thursday, you can try essential oils, perfumes, or creams of rosemary, sandalwood, lime, and dandelion.

Smoothies are a delicious way to improve your health and the recipes are endless. Two foods that appeal to my Heart and throat chakras are kale and blueberries. Both of these foods have a wealth of antioxidants and the sweetness of the blueberries pairs well with the kale. If your tastebuds fancy it, you can blend in other ingredients such as ginger, honey, or banana.

Take some time to process matters of the heart. Maybe there are some niggling parts of your relationship that need resolving or maybe it's time for a much-needed date night. Hug those you love and remind them how much they mean to you. Naturally, this doesn't have to be reserved for Thursdays but if you feel it's been a while, it's good to make Thursdays a love hormone top-up!

Friday

Venus/ Throat Chakra/ Third Eye Chakra/ Pure White

In astrology, Venus plays a direct role in the health of your throat and the throat glands and today is the day to work on effective communication. If you have woken up with that Friday feeling, now is the chance to sing your favorite songs, wake up the vocal cords, and stimulate the vagus nerve.

Venus is pure white, unlike the pale white of the Moon. Both contain all the colors of the spectrum but because this is a bright white, the color is considered to be sophisticated over the simplicity of the Moon. This is why diamond, as a symbol of purity, is often associated with Venus and Fridays. If you are fortunate to have real diamonds, this is a good day to wear them. I am happy with my cubic zirconia. An alternative is the interesting Malachite with its swirling bands of greens. It is said that this crystal of Venus can absorb negative energy and help tap into intuition. You can combine these crystals with Ylang-Ylang, vanilla, chamomile, or apple blossom essential oils. Chamomile is particularly useful to soothe the throat as a herbal tea.

Fruit is ideal for the throat chakra and aside from the purple/blue berries, I like a salad made up of fruits such as apples, pears, and plums but any fruit that can be picked off trees can help healing. The fruits can be mixed with coconut water or a sweet treat with some honey, both good for the throat.

If you haven't quite found your voice but you feel like there are feelings that need to be expressed, take a moment to write them down. This can help to organize thoughts and feelings ready for communication.

Saturday

Saturn/ Third Eye Chakra/ Root Chakra/ Black

It's worth mentioning, the further up the chakras, the weaker the tie with one planet and the closer connection with various planets and their elements. Here is a good example of how. Monday is a good day to practice third eye chakra healing because of the ties to the wisdom of the Moon. Saturn is actually most associated with the root chakra, about grounded practicality, it's a good day to cleanse your home. But Saturn is a wonderful link between the physical and the spiritual. Saturn is the threshold between the planets visible to the naked eye and those that aren't. The two chakras complement each other well, the third eye chakra enables psychic abilities but the root chakra keeps us grounded.

For me, I connect with Black obsidian. Saturn is associated with black because of the absence of light. Too much black can darken the soul, it is also a color that can be calming because of its protective qualities. This stone can also clear away negative energies. And to complete the connection between the two chakras, Saturn, and the color black, this crystal also has grounding properties. You may want to try using patchouli, pine, and myrrh in aromatherapy.

As I have more time on Saturdays, it makes sense to do some baking and for my Third Chakra, I like cinnamon and walnut muffins. Cinnamon is said to increase intuition and walnuts are good for a healthy brain with Omega 3 and antioxidants. Because it's baking, the ingredients need to be a little more precise so I will add my recipe.

- 2 cups of all-purpose flour
- ¾ cup of granulated sugar
- ¾ cup of milk
- ½ cup of salted butter
- ½ cup of chopped walnuts
- 2 large eggs
- 2 teaspoons of baking powder
- 1 tablespoon of ground cinnamon
- 1 apple peeled and cut into small cubes (optional)

Preheat the oven to 350°F. Melt the butter and mix all of the liquid ingredients together and then add the sugar. In a separate bowl, mix the dry ingredients together before adding them to the liquid ingredients. Add the walnuts and optional apple. You can sprinkle a little extra sugar and cinnamon over the muffins before baking them if you want. They take about 20 minutes to cook.

After cleansing your house, take a moment to make a manifestation or goal box. Add items and pictures that help give you a tangible reminder of what you are working towards.

Sunday

Sun/ Crown Chakra

In reality, you will be able to feel some form of connection to many planets when working on the crown chakra but as the last day of the week and the power of the Sun, it keeps things a little simpler. To give you an idea of other planetary connections, Jupiter is the planet of expansion, the moon governs our instincts, and Uranus frees us from mental blocks and gives us access to powerful insights beyond the mundane.

When using the sun for your crown chakra, begin your day by pulling back the drapes and letting that light flood your room, lay back down on the bed and meditate. It's like starting your day with some solar power and if the weather is right, open the window for some fresh air.

Sunstone holds the power of solar light; it radiates warmth and strength and can help improve our stamina. Orange stones are also helpful for the crown chakra.

These stones can be left in the sun for 6 to 24 hours in order to charge them. You can pair your crystal work with amber, marigold, and juniper essential oils.

There are two ways to nourish your crown chakra. The first way is to detox the body and remove those toxins that impact the body and mind. Lemon and turmeric are good for the liver, and so is milk thistle. The other way is to increase your intake of sun-dried foods. Most fruits and vegetables can be sun-dried and herbs are super easy. You can try adding sun-dried tomatoes and saffron to your favorite pasta dishes.

It's a good day to spend a little time decluttering your home. A cluttered home leads to a cluttered mind and added stress you don't need. It's harder to appreciate spiritual awareness when mental clutter is holding you back.

The point of this chapter was not to confuse you with conflicting planets, colors, and more crystals. Instead, it was to emphasize the fact that there is no right or wrong way to work on balancing your chakras. The only way that you can really go wrong is by ignoring the symptoms of imbalance in the chakras. Along your journey, you will try techniques that have a resounding impact on your well-being and others that don't seem to do anything. It's helpful to keep a journal of the differences your practices make and tweak your weekly plan so that it's full of wonderful activities that leave you feeling mentally and physically revitalized.

Your Good Deed of the Day!

As an author deeply passionate about self-healing topics, I believe this book holds valuable insights for those seeking to unlock their inner potential and foster overall well-being.

Your feedback is of immense importance to me. I kindly request your genuine review of "Chakra Healing and the Vagus Nerve," highlighting its strengths, areas for improvement, and any personal experiences gained.

To leave a review, please consider visiting the book's Amazon page by clicking on the link below or scanning the QR code:

https://www.amazon.com/review/create-review/?ie=UTF8&channel=glance-detail&asin=B0CD4G1W4H

Conclusion

Self-care is something busy moms are guilty of neglecting, in fact, on a larger scale, it's something that we could all do with a little more of regardless of age or gender. There just aren't enough hours in the day to get everything done. It feels like in order to prioritize our own needs, a bigger sacrifice has to be made.

After taking a closer look at the importance of creating balance within the chakras, there is one major takeaway I hope you gained. Healing and taking care of yourself only needs a few minutes a day and some greater self-awareness.

Despite the fact that there is little science behind the chakras, it doesn't mean that the practices involved in balancing them haven't been proven. As science continues to progress and dedicate time to researching ancient practices, we are more aware of how something as simple as deep, intentional breathing can dramatically reduce the effects of stress on the body and mind. Visualization is a technique used by people from all warps of life from actors to athletes. Yoga has immense benefits for the physical body and yoga therapy has been shown to improve mental health.

And then there is the vagus nerve. To me, it feels like this magical nerve is the body's best kept secret and although medical professionals will obviously have a good knowledge of vagal tone, when we lay people are able to learn about its role in our health and simple ways to stimulate it, we can take huge steps to controlling our own health better.

There is plenty of evidence to support vagus nerve stimulation and the nervous system. Once again, you can compare the advances in vagus nerve understanding to the advances in mindfulness and meditation. For years, we have been telling ourselves to count to ten and breathe deeply. We may have thought that splashing cold water on your face was recycled advice, just something to take our mind off the problem at hand. But these techniques that have been used for generations before us are highly effective.

What's exciting is the research that is ongoing. Scientists are looking into how mindfulness can be as effective as pain medication and there is research into vagus nerve stimulation to help manage symptoms of ADHD. The more we can learn about alternative and holistic approaches, the less need there may be for pharmaceuticals and their potential side effects.

When we combine vagus nerve stimulation with other essential practices we have seen from Eastern philosophies, working on balancing your chakras through these traditional and proven practices can have a mind-blowing effect on your well-being.

You may have a specific health concern that you are hoping to address and would like to turn straight to that chakra, which is fine, but it is well-advised to combine different strategies that encourage energy to flow to all of the chakras considering they are all intertwined. Without wanting to sound repetitive, my weekly schedule suits me and it makes me feel good. If you discover the same results by following it, that's wonderful, but if you want to tweak it or even create your own plan entirely, that's great too. Just try to aim for consistency and a little bit each day.

In my opinion, understanding the chakras has proven invaluable for my holistic approach to improving my physical and emotional health. Discovering more about each chakra has enabled me to learn more about my strengths and weaknesses and to focus my attention on areas of my well-being that need more attention.

All too often we talk about a lack of energy and look for quick fixes to recuperate some of our lost energy. For most, it will be a boost of caffeine, a sugar rush, or an early night. But these are often just short-term solutions for bigger, underlying issues. By beginning with the root chakra, you can begin to feel more grounded and stable in life, something that many of have probably lacked over the last few years. Working your way up the spine, you can understand more about any issues with your digestive and reproductive systems.

While no chakra is more important than the next, when the heart chakra and the throat chakra are balanced, you can see life-changing results in your relationships in terms of emotional awareness and expression. This isn't just limited to your relationships with others. For our own mental health, it's essential that people learn how to create a more positive relationship with themselves, discovering more about goals and desires, even the direction to take in life.

You too can pinpoint your physical and emotional needs, make the necessary changes, and allow pure energy to flow through you without the need for temporary fixes. This isn't about waking up one day feeling revitalized, it's about waking up every day with the same vigor and vest for life!

You may have done some research and wondered why I have never used the word open when referring to chakras. Opening the chakras can often be a process that is too fast and too soon, especially when dealing with emotions. Open chakras can lead to becoming more aware of negativity and suffering. Much like how we have seen the effects of an underactive and overactive chakra, we want them to be neither blocked nor wide up to let excessive amounts of energy through. The key will always be balance!

Please take care with yoga poses. Generally speaking, yoga is safe for everybody, regardless of your current levels of fitness or age. If you are new to yoga or you have concerns about your stability, feel free to use a chair for support until you gain some experience. Remember that yoga should cause you to feel stretches in your joints and muscles but it should never cause you pain. Pain means you are overstretching your body, ease up a bit. With time, your body will become stronger and more flexible. If you are pregnant or have any health conditions, please check with your doctor before beginning yoga.

Balancing your chakras doesn't depend on yoga, so don't force yourself to do something that won't lead to happiness. Exploring chakras and integrating practices into your daily life is a fascinating way to learn more about yourself and the world around you. There is now nothing in between you and igniting your inner potential, overcoming obstacles and barriers, and leading a fulfilling, peaceful life!

Like you, are so many people who are skeptical of chakra healing or don't know enough about it to fully appreciate its worth. If I could ask one small favor of you, I would be eternally grateful if you could share your opinions on Amazon. This way, more people can discover that they are able to change their lives for the better by learning about these powerful energy wheels. Together, we can help others to lead a happy life, something that the world really needs right now!

Good luck and I look forward to hearing about your experiences!

References

4 scientific facts about mindfulness that prove its transformative effects on us. (n.d.). Aura. https://www.aurahealth.io/blog/4-scientific-facts-about-mindfulness-that-prove-its-transformative-effects-on-us#:~:text=Mindfulness%20physically%20rebuilds%20your%20brain&text=Astonishingly%2C%20the%20research%20found%20an,connected%20to%20anxiety%20and%20stress.

Dreher, D. E. (2018, October 29). *Surprising research on the color blue*. Psychology Today. https://www.psychologytoday.com/intl/blog/your-personal-renaissance/201810/surprising-research-the-color-blue

Menigoz, W., Latz, T. T., Ely, R. J., Kamei, C., Melvin, G., & Sinatra, D. (2020). Integrative and lifestyle medicine strategies should include Earthing (grounding): Review of research evidence and clinical observations. *Explore-the Journal of Science and Healing*, *16*(3), 152–160. https://doi.org/10.1016/j.explore.2019.10.005

Naghdi, L., Ahonen, H., Macario, P., & Bartel, L. (2015). The effect of Low-Frequency sound stimulation on patients with fibromyalgia: A clinical study. *Pain Research & Management*, *20*(1), e21–e27. https://doi.org/10.1155/2015/375174

Peachman, R. (2017, August 3). Electrical grounding technique may improve health outcomes of NICU babies. *Penn State University*. https://www.psu.edu/news/research/story/electrical-grounding-technique-may-improve-health-outcomes-nicu-babies/

Penn Medicine. (2016, March 17). *How yoga benefits the heart.*
https://www.pennmedicine.org/updates/blogs/heart-and-vascular-blog/2016/march/how-yoga-benefits-the-heart

Team, S., Team, S., & SingleCare. (2023). Stress statistics 2023: How common is stress and who's most affected? *The Checkup.*
https://www.singlecare.com/blog/news/stress-statistics/

www.ingramcontent.com/pod-product-compliance
Lightning Source LLC
Chambersburg PA
CBHW072057110526
44590CB00018B/3208